Lollipop Logic

Lollipop Logic employs visual and pictorial clues to introduce and reinforce high-powered thinking for pre-readers.

Seven different thinking skills—sequences, relationships, analogies, deduction, pattern decoding, inference, and critical analysis—are presented in a format designed to appeal to gifted young learners. This straightforward, one-of-a-kind tool gives wings to pre-readers and non-readers who are ready for a challenge but don't yet have the reading skills for more traditional critical thinking activities.

Now with full-color illustrations, this beloved classic has been fully updated with refreshed activities, images, and text to help young learners continue to soar into the stratosphere of thinking skills far beyond their reading levels.

Bonnie and **Rob Risby** are a mother-and-son team that has been co-authoring books since the 1980s. Bonnie has been a teacher of French, English, and Gifted and Talented Education; a psychotherapist specializing in family and couples counselling; an author; and a businesswoman. Rob is a winner of the *Learning Magazine's* Teachers' Choice 1994 Award for Excellence in Classroom Products for a two-book series on map skills.

Critical Thinking Activities
(Book 2, Grades K-2)

Lollipop Logic

Second Edition

Bonnie Risby &
Robert K. Risby, II

Routledge
Taylor & Francis Group

NEW YORK AND LONDON

Designed cover image: Raquel Trevino

Second edition published 2024
by Routledge
605 Third Avenue, New York, NY 10158

and by Routledge
4 Park Square, Milton Park, Abingdon, Oxon, OX14 4RN

Routledge is an imprint of the Taylor & Francis Group, an informa business

First edition published by Prufrock Press 2011

Library of Congress Cataloging-in-Publication Data
Names: Risby, Bonnie Lou, author. | Risby, Robert K., II, author.
Title: Lollipop logic : critical thinking activities (book 2, grades K-2) /
Bonnie Risby & Robert K. Risby, II.
Description: Second edition. | New York : Routledge, 2024. |
"First edition published by Prufrock Press 2011"–T.p.verso. | Audience: Grades K-2 |
Summary: – Provided by publisher.
Identifiers: LCCN 2023018936 (print) | LCCN 2023018937 (ebook) |
ISBN 9781032480671 (hbk) | ISBN 9781032469805 (pbk) |
ISBN 9781003387213 (ebk)
Subjects: LCSH: Critical thinking–Problems, exercises, etc.–Juvenile literature. |
Reasoning–Problems, exercises, etc.–Juvenile literature. |
Logic–Problems, exercises, etc.–Juvenile literature.
Classification: LCC LB1590.3 .R628 2024 (print) | LCC LB1590.3 (ebook) |
DDC 372.47/4–dc23/eng/20230519
LC record available at https://lccn.loc.gov/2023018936
LC ebook record available at https://lccn.loc.gov/2023018937

ISBN: 978-1-032-48067-1 (hbk)
ISBN: 978-1-032-46980-5 (pbk)
ISBN: 978-1-003-38721-3 (ebk)

DOI: 10.4324/9781003387213

Typeset in Warnock Pro
by Newgen Publishing UK

Contents

About this Book

Lollipop Logic is designed to present critical thinking skills to young students who may not yet have mastered reading skills. In the past, these skills have been reserved for much older students; however, there is nothing lacking in the development of very young students to prohibit introducing and nurturing these skills other than a degree of reading proficiency. *Lollipop Logic* is unique in that it combines problems involving deduction, analogies, relationships, sequencing, pattern decoding, inference, and critical analyzing skills in a format designed to appeal to students in grades K to 2 without any reading barrier. As young children develop these thinking skills, expect to see them approach all materials with critical forethought.

To the Teacher

Lollipop Logic is the direct result of requests by educators for lessons presenting critical thinking skills in a format suitable for younger students. The teacher is indeed the most important element in making critical thinking skills work for younger students. It is the instructor's role not only to present the process, but also to foster an atmosphere where creative and critical thinking are encouraged and any fear of failure is absent. Because the thought process itself is more important than the answers provided in the back of the book, it is very important to discuss and compare methods that students use to arrive at conclusions and to be tolerant of creative diversions from the norm. It is suggested that each new type of skill be presented and discussed and that sample problems be worked together before students are challenged to work independently.

Skills Presented in this Book

Sequences. Sequencing problems require students to look at time relationships. Pictorial sequences presented here require young thinkers to look at a group of illustrations to determine the relationship before selecting the item that must come first, the one coming second, and so forth. They must study the illustrations to discover the relationship that dictates the sequence. They should always be encouraged to take care to correct any error that would create subsequent errors in the sequencing pattern.

Relationships. In this section, students will be looking for ways that certain things relate to one another. Some of the relationships will be obvious; others will be more subtle. Students should be reminded to be flexible and creative and not to become alarmed when the relationship they define is different than one discovered by their neighbors. Exercises in this section should be completed before introducing analogies, as analogical thinking is based on being able to identify relationships.

Analogies. Analogies are comparisons between things based on similar characteristics. This section contains both figural and pictorial analogies that are very similar to the literal or verbal analogies undertaken by older students. Although first attempts may be awkward, young children usually catch on to analogies quite readily find them challenging, and relate to them with the adventurousness of one learning a new sport. To solve the analogies, students must find the relationship between the first two items and then establish the same or a very similar relationship between a second pair of items that completes the analogy It would be helpful to go through several examples together before beginning individual work.

Deduction. Deduction is a form of inference in which the conclusion follows from premises or statements of fact. Since we are targeting a nonreading population, we have endeavored to keep the clues extremely brief. Teachers should read the clues clearly, repeat them carefully, and then allow the learner adequate time to solve the problem by logically linking together all of the facts.

Pattern Decoding. Exercises in pattern decoding present a series of figures that represent a pattern. Students are to study the illustrations to discover the pattern. Once they have discovered the pattern, they are to select one other illustration that would come next in the pattern. There are several skills that come into play in these exercises. Students must be able to distinguish between the visual images, recognize the pattern that is presented, and forecast what the next element in the sequence will be. If students encounter trouble in completing the pattern, it may be necessary to go back and review one or more aspects of this skill.

Inference. The use of inference is a broad area of logic. Inference involves reaching conclusions from gathered evidence. It means going from the known to the unknown and forming educated guesses based on either facts or premises. This book includes pictorial exercises to introduce students to inference based thinking. They must critically examine the pictorial evidence presented and proceed to the next logical step or to the conclusion that is required.

Critical Analysis. Critical analyzing skills involve examining given information and reaching conclusions from gathered evidence. This process is very similar to one of the oldest logic arguments, syllogisms. The young thinkers are presented with two groups of items, represented entirely with pictures, to carefully scrutinize and analyze. They know the following:

- *All members of group A are Z.*
- *All members of group B are not Z.*

Then they are presented with new items to examine and determine whether or not they are Z. The pictures in both groups are nonsensical. They do, however, establish valid relationships that will lead to and support conclusions.

Teacher's Instructions

Sequences (Lessons 1–8)

Note: For all sequencing lessons, caution students against marking the blanks too quickly without careful consideration. Remind them that an error in an early step of the solution could cause subsequent errors.

Lesson 1: Preface this exercise in sequencing by explaining that a spider is spinning its web. Each picture represents a logical step that must either precede or follow another sequential step. Explain that there is only one logically acceptable solution, so students must consider the order very carefully. Students should label the first step in the sequence 1, the second 2, and so on.

Lesson 2: Explain that the following pictures show sand passing through an hourglass. Ask students to carefully consider which picture comes first, and then place a 1 in the blank by that picture. They should place a 2 by the picture that comes second, and so forth. Be sure that students realize there is only one correct sequence.

Lesson 3: Preface this exercise in sequencing by explaining that a candle is about to be lit and then melt. Students will see six pictures representing the different stages of the candle melting. Explain that there is only one logically acceptable solution, so students must carefully consider the order of the pictures. Students should number the pictures in the order in which they will happen.

Lesson 4: Instruct the students that what they are about to see is six views of the same piggy bank. The piggy bank starts out empty, but by the end, its owner has lots of coins. By carefully considering the pictures, students can determine whether each of the six pictures precedes or follows another picture in the sequence. Explain that there is only one logically acceptable solution, so students must carefully consider the order of the pictures. Students should number the pictures in the order in which they will happen.

Lesson 5: Preface this exercise in sequencing by explaining that someone is blowing up a balloon. Students will see six pictures representing progressive stages of the balloon getting bigger—perhaps even escaping from the person blowing it up. Explain that there is only one logically acceptable solution, so they must carefully consider the order of the pictures. Students should number the pictures to show the order in which they will happen.

Lesson 6: Preface this exercise in sequencing by explaining that a seed has been planted in the soil. Students will see six pictures representing progressive stages from germination of the seed to its growth into a mature plant. Explain that there is only one logically acceptable solution, so students must carefully consider the order of the pictures. Students should number the pictures in the order they think they will happen.

Lesson 7: Preface this exercise in sequencing by explaining that someone is performing on the high dive. The pictures students are about to see will represent the progressive stages of the diver reaching the platform and leaping into a pool. Explain that there is only one logically acceptable solution, so students must carefully consider the order of the pictures. Students should number the pictures according to the order in which they will happen.

Lesson 8: Explain to students that they are going to see several pictures showing a pizza being eaten. Explain that there is only one logically acceptable solution, so students must carefully consider the order of the pictures. Students should number the pictures according to the order in which they will happen.

Relationships (Lessons 9–16)

Lessons 9–12: All of the lessons in this section have the same instructions. Read the following instructions to students.

> *Look at the first thing in the row, the thing that is in the small box. It has something in common with one of the three things in the big box next to it. It could be that they are the same shape, the same design, the same size, or are alike in some other way. Find the picture that is most like the first picture and draw a circle around it.*

Lessons 13–16: All of the lessons in this section have the same instructions. Read the following instructions to students.

> *A group of things that belong together are in the box. Look at the items in this group carefully to determine what they have in common or why they belong together. Then look carefully at the items below the box and decide if they could belong with the items in the boxed group. If they do belong to the group of things in the box, draw a circle around them. If they do not belong to the group, draw an X through them.*

Analogies (Lessons 17–24)

Analogies are comparisons between two sets of things. They compare features that are not always obvious. Approach these pictorial and figural analogies with very young learners by carefully examining and talking about the examples given. Remember, this is a completely new concept for these young individuals. Don't be discouraged by awkward first attempts. Also, remember that it is the process itself that we want to instill, so working in groups and sharing with the class are good initial approaches.

Lessons 17–19: For each of these lessons, read the following instructions to students.

Look at the two things in the first box. Think about how they are related. Then look at the picture to the right of the box. One of the three choices is related to this thing in the same way the first two things are related. Find the one thing that is related to the third thing in the same way the first two things are related. Draw a circle around this thing.

Lessons 20–24: For all of these lessons, read the following instructions to students.

Look at the first two pictures. Think about how they are related. Then look for the two pictures underneath the top two pictures that are related to each other in the same way. Circle the correct pair.

Deduction (Lessons 25–31)

The activities in this section are designed with the prereader in mind; however, listening comprehension is required. Also, the student must be able to distinguish the four characters in the activity. The figures are labeled, but some learners may wish to color the characters or code them in some other manner. Read the problem and clues slowly and distinctly, pause to allow thinking, and reread clues. This presentation can be repeated as many times as necessary. If students are working in pairs or small groups, allow them enough time to discuss their solutions. Have students draw a line from each character to the item with which that character is associated.

Lesson 25 – Chopsticks and Fortune Cookies: Sebastian, Evan, Emma, and Falon all ordered takeout from a Chinese menu. They ordered potstickers, shrimp fried rice, sushi, and noodle soup. Listen carefully to the clues, and then draw a line connecting each person with what he or she bought.

Clues:
1. Emma said the girl ordering shrimp fried rice both had cookies containing identical fortunes.
2. Evan and his friend Sebastian ordered sushi and potstickers and were very excited to try using chopsticks.
3. Evan did not order the potstickers.

Lesson 26 – Prism Crayon Company: Sydney, Lydia, Rob, and Tyler all participated in a poll sponsored by the Prism Crayon Company. Each child was asked to use the new colors from the company, and then to pick his or her two favorites. The color pairs chosen were: hummingbird green/red velvet; watermelon pink/robin's-egg blue; mulberry purple/jack-o-lantern orange; and swallowtail yellow/cedar green. Listen carefully to the clues, and then draw a line connecting each person with the color that he or she picked.

Clues:
1. Rob and Sydney both had a shade of green in their pair of favorite colors.
2. Tyler and the girl choosing watermelon pink had a hard time choosing only two colors.
3. Sydney did not choose red velvet.

Lesson 27 – Hiking Snacks: Crystal, Julie, Nick, and Clayton all hiked the Chipmunk Trail at White Oak Park. Halfway through the hike, they took a break to share their snacks: string cheese; apple slices; juice pouches; and strawberry leather. Listen carefully to the clues, and then draw a line connecting each person with the snack he or she carried in a backpack.

Clues:
1. Nick and the boy who brought juice to share were glad to empty their backpacks.
2. Crystal and the girl sharing apple slices also brought wipes and napkins to share.
3. Nick did not bring the strawberry leather.

Lesson 28 – Vacation on the Coast: Grandma Tonia, Grandpa Dave, Becky, and Sebastian took a vacation to the Georgia Coast. Their stay was very enjoyable, and each person had a favorite memory: collecting shells at low tide; visiting the turtle sanctuary; identifying birds in the salt marshes; and bumping into former President Jimmy Carter at a seafood restaurant. Listen carefully to the clues, and then draw a line connecting each person with his or her favorite vacation memory.

Clues:
1. Sebastian and his mom visited the beach at low tide and also visited the turtle sanctuary.
2. Grandma Tonia loved sitting on the balcony early in the morning, when the birds became active in the marshes.
3. Becky is not the person whose favorite memory was the turtle sanctuary.

Lesson 29 – The Birthday Album: Dakota, Taylor, Logan, and Jackson are making a combined birthday album-scrapbook. Each friend contributes photos and mementos from his or her birthday, held at one of the following places: the Water Park; the Bouncing Air Arcade; the Magic Park; and the Victorian Doll Museum. Listen carefully to the clues, and then draw a line connecting each person to his or her birthday celebration.

Clues:
1. Dakota and the girl who celebrated at the quaint tearoom and the adjoining Victorian Doll Museum invited both boys and girls to their parties.
2. Jackson and the boy who loved bouncing at the Air Arcade both celebrate birthdays during the same month.
3. Dakota is not the person who celebrated at the Magic Park.

Lesson 30 – Lavender Farm: Chloe, Kaitlyn, Aidan, and London visit the Lavender Farm. They all spend a wonderful afternoon there. Each person leaves with a different favorite memory: gathering bundles of lavender; sampling lavender lemonade and jelly; crafting lavender wreaths; and making lavender cookies. Listen carefully to the clues, and then draw a line connecting each person with his or her favorite Lavender Farm memory.

Clues:
1. Chloe and the girl who spent most of her time gathering lavender planned to make sachets for gifts.
2. Aidan and the boy who enjoyed the lavender lemonade and jelly were amazed at how gentle the honeybees were that worked in the lavender fields among the people gathering the wonderful-smelling stems.
3. Chloe is **not** the one who enjoyed making lavender cookies.

Lesson 31 – County Fair: Shannon, Tasha, Colby, and Adam attend the county fair near their homes. While wandering the fairgrounds, they each have a different favorite activity: fishing for prizes; going down the giant slide; eating funnel cake; and putting golf balls at a target. Listen carefully to the clues, and then draw a line connecting each person to his or her favorite county fair activity.

Clues:
1. Colby and the boy who could putt golf balls through a narrow opening stayed for the evening fireworks.
2. Shannon and the girl who loved fishing for plastic ducks to win prizes had 25 tickets each.
3. Colby did **not** like funnel cake.

Pattern Decoding (Lessons 32–39)

All of the lessons in this section have the same instructions. Read the following instructions to the students. (Note that some items in the answer list may be used more than once, and some may not be used at all.)

Study the following patterns carefully. After you find the pattern, choose the item from the answer list that should come next. Draw a line connecting the pattern to the item in the list that should come next.

Inference (Lessons 40–49)

Lessons 40–41: Read the following instructions to students.

Each of the pictures below has a part that is missing. The missing parts are shown along the side of the page. Find the missing part of each picture. Draw a line between the picture and its missing section.

Lessons 42–43: Read the following instructions to students.

Each picture has a missing piece. Beside it are several pieces that could fit in the place of the missing piece. Only one piece will fit to correctly complete the picture. Choose the correct missing piece. Draw a circle around it.

Lessons 44–45: Read the following instructions to students.

Below are some pieces to a puzzle. Some of the pieces are missing. By carefully examining the pieces below, you can get an idea of what the total picture is. After you know what the puzzle represents, draw the picture on a separate piece of paper.

Lessons 46–47: Read the following instructions to students.

The left side shows several different pictures. On the right side, there are more pictures. Each picture on the left side is related to a picture on the right side in some way. Draw a line between each picture on the left and the picture on the right that it is most related to or goes with best.

Lessons 48–49: Read the following instructions for all lessons.

There are six different drawings on this page. The drawings show only part of a larger drawing. Look at this part carefully and see if you can guess what the whole picture would look like. Describe what you think this is a picture of.

Critical Analysis (Lessons 50–52)

Lessons 50–52: Read the following instructions, selecting the figure name that corresponds to the lesson.

Several species of new life forms have been discovered on the planet Olympianus. See if you can identify them. The top row shows things that are leemoys/shootles/beltazoids. The next row shows things that are not leemoys/shootles/beltazoids. Look at the creatures on the bottom and decide whether they are leemoys/shootles/beltazoids or not. If they are, draw a circle around them. If they are not, draw an X through them. Look back at the examples as often as you like.

Reproducible Lessons

Sequences

Lessons 1–8

Lesson 1

Number these pictures to show the correct order.

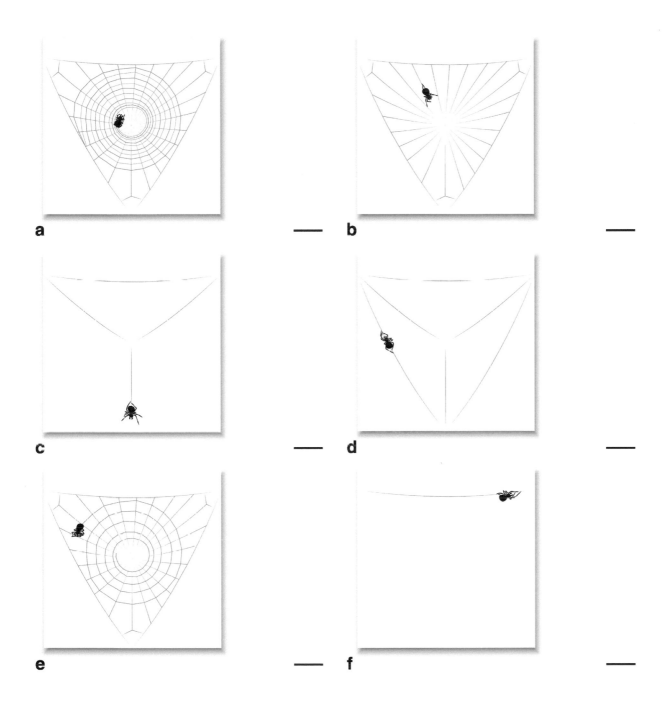

a   ___   b   ___

c   ___   d   ___

e   ___   f   ___

Number these pictures to show the correct order.

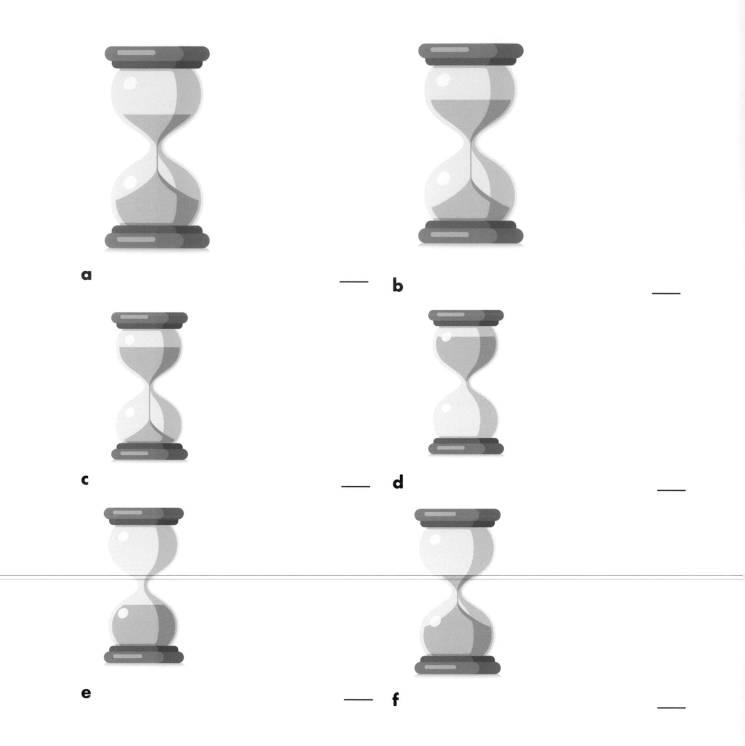

a

b ___

___

c

d ___

___

e

f ___

___

Lesson 3

Number these pictures to show the correct order.

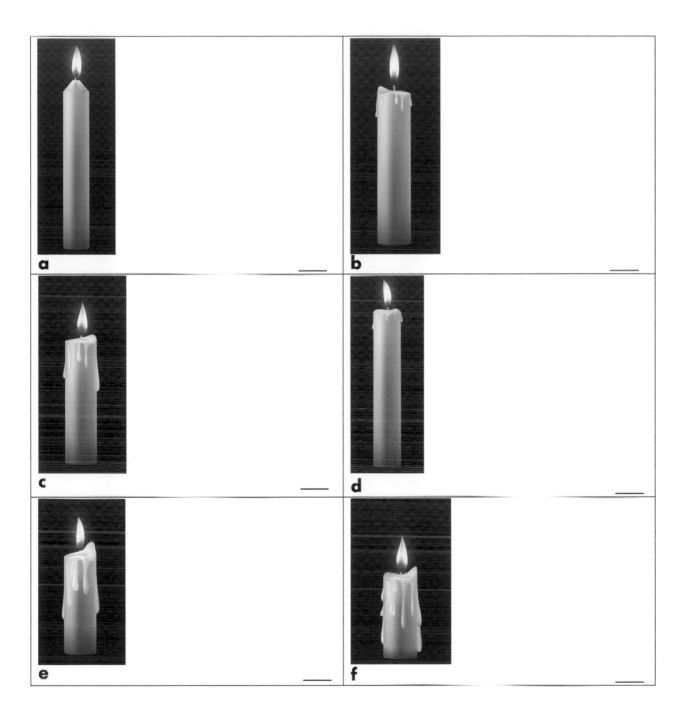

a _____   b _____

c _____   d _____

e _____   f _____

Lesson 4

Number these pictures to show the correct order.

a   _____

b   _____

c   _____

d   _____

e   _____

f   _____

Number these pictures to show the correct order.

a   _____ b   _____

c   _____ d   _____

e   _____ f   _____

Lesson 6

Number these pictures to show the correct order.

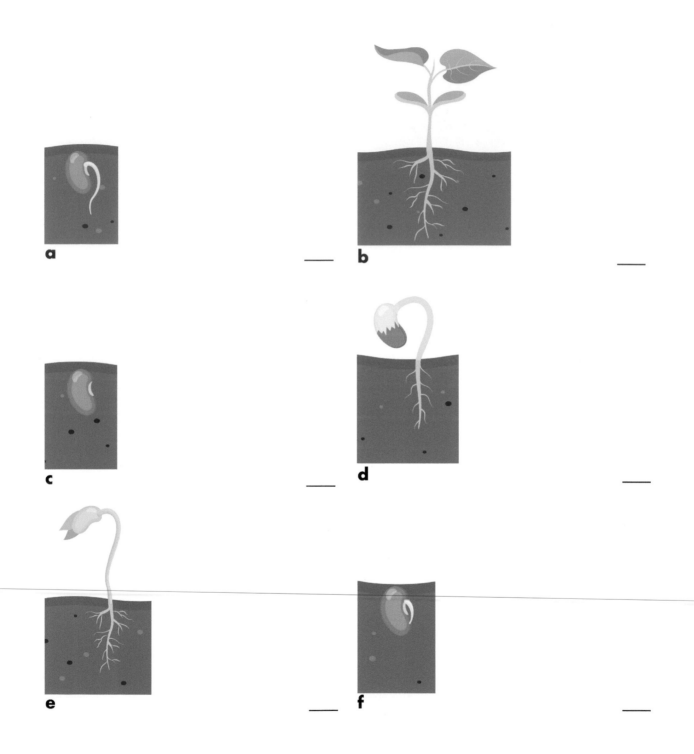

a

b _____ _____

c

d _____ _____

e

f _____ _____

Lesson 7

Number these pictures to show the correct order.

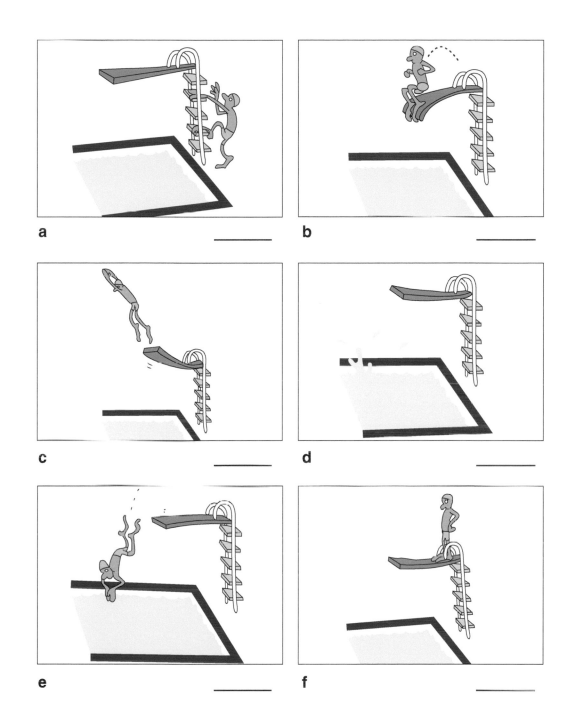

a _____ b _____

c _____ d _____

e _____ f _____

Number these pictures to show the correct order.

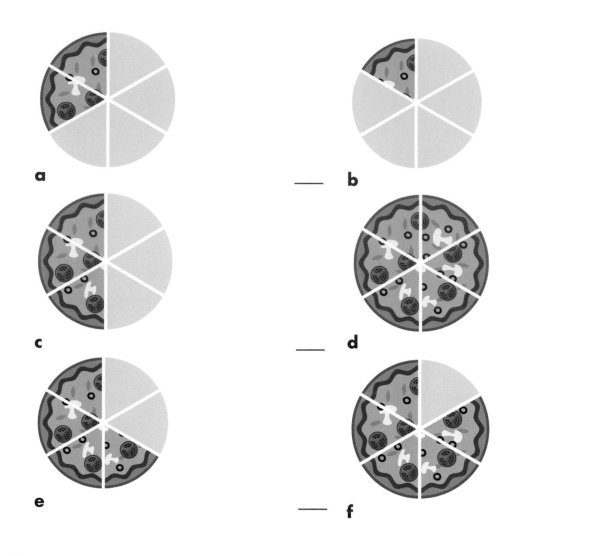

a

_____ b _____

c

_____ d _____

e

_____ f _____

Relationships

Lessons 9–16

Lesson 9

Draw a circle around the picture that has something in common with the first picture.

Copyright material from Risby (2024), *Lollipop Logic Book 2*, Routledge

DOI: 10.4324/9781003387213-2

Lesson 10

Draw a circle around the picture that has something in common with the first picture.

Draw a circle around the picture that has something in common with the first picture.

Lesson 12

Draw a circle around the picture that has something in common with the first picture.

There is a group of related things in the box. Circle the things on this page that belong in the group. Put an X through the things that do not belong in the group.

Lesson 14

There is a group of related things in the box. Circle the things on this page that belong in the group. Put an X through the things that do not belong in the group.

There is a group of related things in the box. Circle the things on this page that belong in the group. Put an X through the things that do not belong in the group.

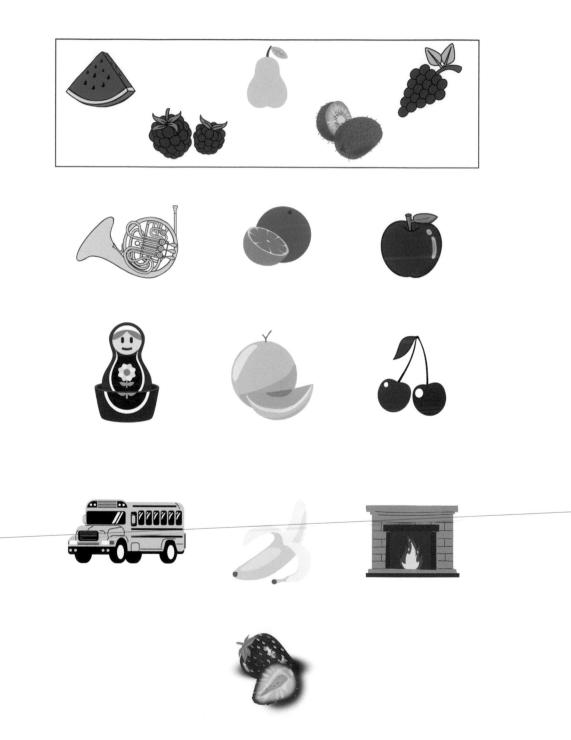

Lesson 16

There is a group of related things in the box. Circle the things on this page that belong in the group. Put an X through the things that do not belong in the group.

Analogies

Lessons 17–24

Lesson 17

Circle the thing that is related to the third thing in the same way the first two things are related.

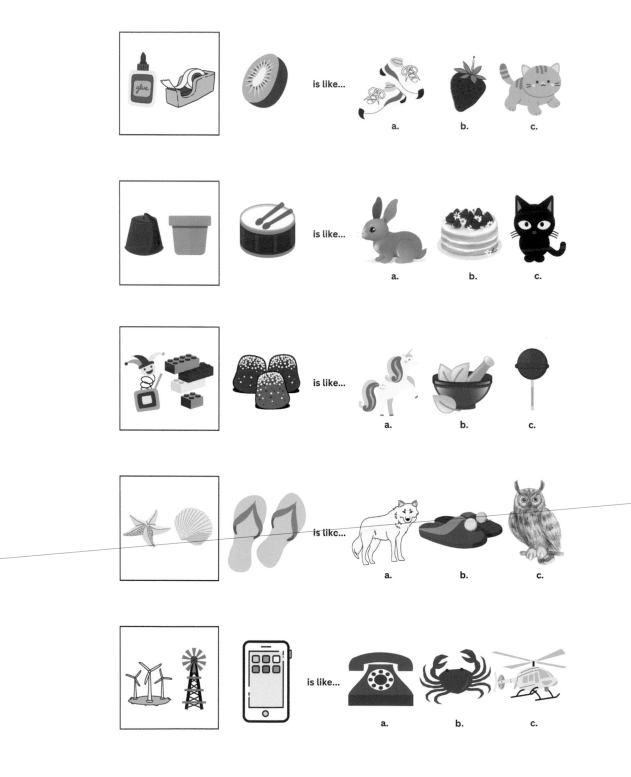

DOI: 10.4324/9781003387213-3

Lesson 18

Circle the thing that is related to the third thing in the same way the first two things are related.

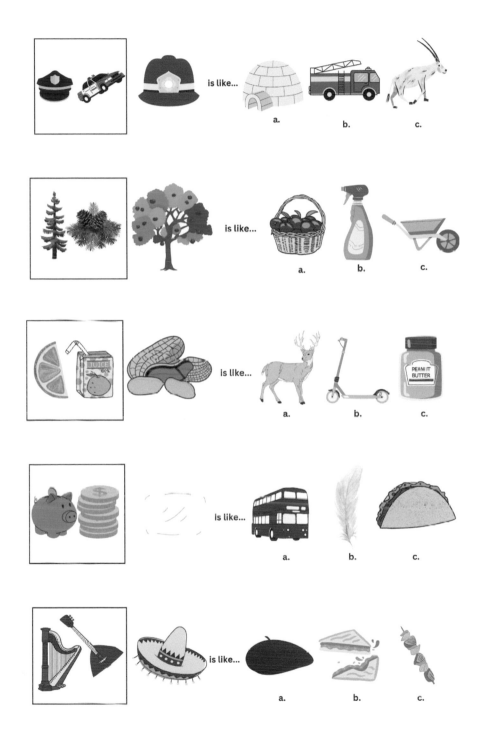

Lesson 19

Circle the thing that is related to the third thing in the same way the first two things are related.

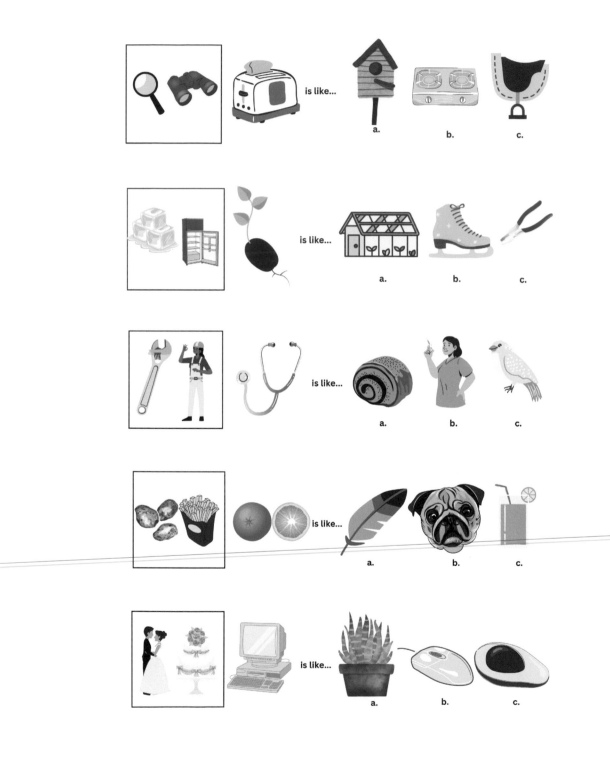

Lesson 20

Choose the pair of pictures that are related to each other in the same way the top two pictures are related. Circle the correct pair.

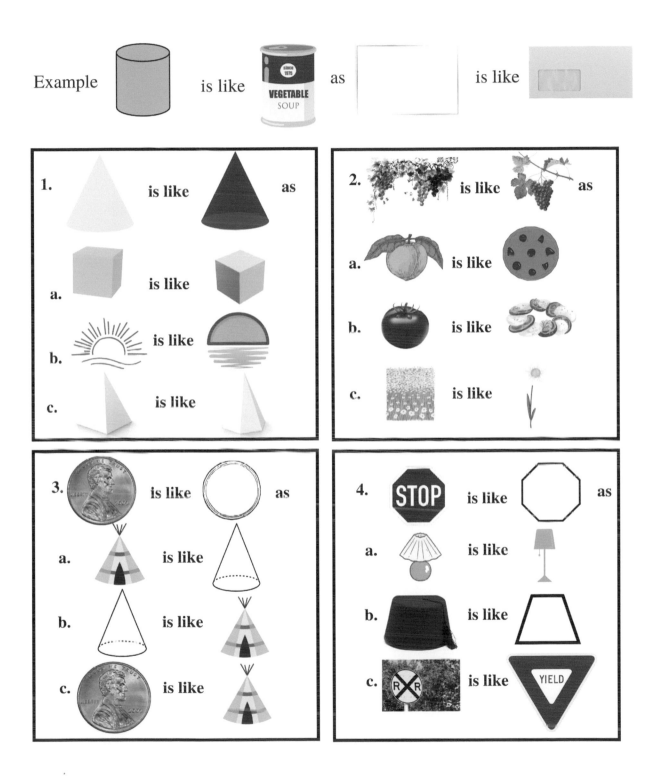

Lesson 21

Choose the pair of pictures that are related to each other in the same way the top two pictures are related. Circle the correct pair.

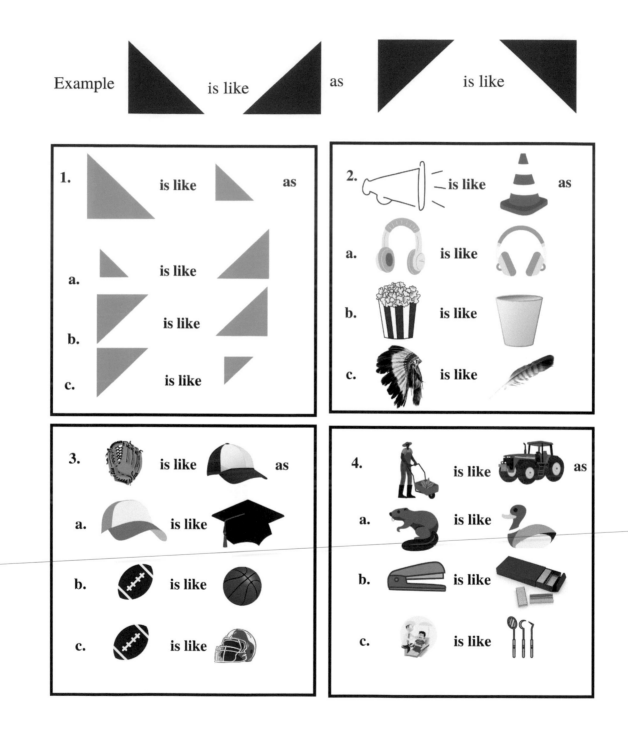

Lesson 22

Choose the pair of pictures that are related to each other in the same way the top two pictures are related. Circle the correct pair.

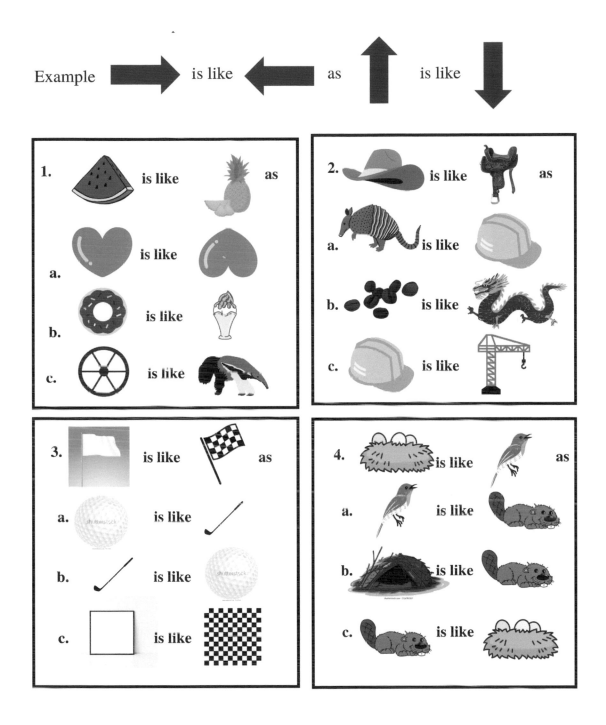

Lesson 23

Choose the pair of pictures that are related to each other in the same way the top two pictures are related. Circle the correct pair.

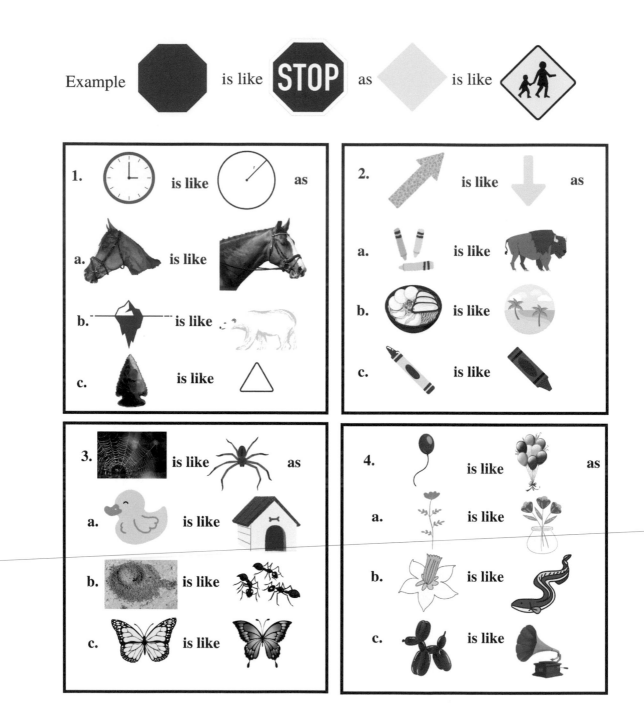

Lesson 24

Choose the pair of pictures that are related to each other in the same way the top two pictures are related. Circle the correct pair.

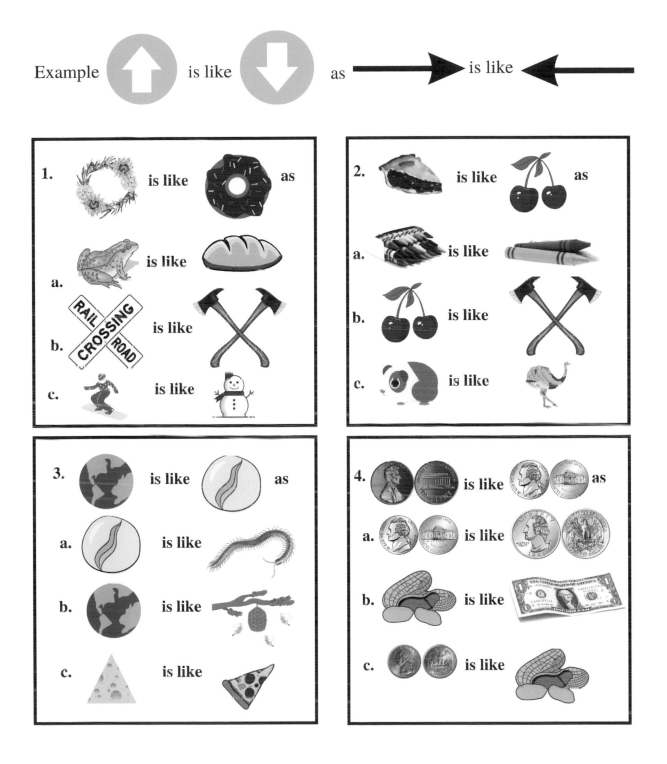

Deduction

Lessons 25–31

Lesson 25

Chopsticks and Fortune Cookies

Sebastian, Evan, Emma, and Falon all ordered takeout from a Chinese menu. They ordered pot stickers, shrimp fried rice, sushi, and noodle soup. Listen carefully to the clues, and then draw a line connecting each person with what he or she bought.

Clues

1. Emma and the girl ordering shrimp fried rice both had cookies containing identical fortunes.
2. Evan and his friend Sebastian ordered sushi and potstickers and were very excited to try using chopsticks.
3. Evan did not order the potstickers

 DOI: 10.4324/9781003387213-4

Lesson 26

Prism Crayon Company

Sydney, Lydia, Rob, and Tyler all participated in a poll sponsored by the Prism Crayon Company. Each child was asked to use the new colors from the company, and then to pick his or her two favorites. The color pairs chosen were: hummingbird green/red velvet; watermelon pink/robin's-egg blue; mulberry purple/jack-o-lantern orange; and swallow-tail yellow/cedar green. Listen carefully to the clues, and then draw a line connecting each person with the two that he or she picked.

Clues
1. Rob and Sydney both had a shade of green in their pair of favorite colors.
2. Tyler and the girl choosing watermelon pink had a hard time choosing only two colors.
3. Sydney did not choose red velvet.

Lesson 27

Hiking Snacks

Crystal, Julie, Nick, and Clayton all hiked the Chipmunk Trail at White Oak Park. Halfway through the hike, they took a break to share their snacks: string cheese; apple slices; juice boxes; and strawberry leather. Listen carefully to the clues, and then draw a line connecting each person with the snack he or she carried in a backpack.

Clues

1. Nick and the boy who brought juice to share were glad to empty their backpacks.
2. Crystal and the girl sharing apple slices also brought wipes and napkins to share.
3. Nick did not bring the strawberry leather.

Vacation on the Coast

Grandma Tonia, Grandpa Dave, Becky, and Sebastian took a vacation to the Georgia Coast. Their stay was very enjoyable, and each person had a favorite memory: collecting shells at low tide; visiting the turtle sanctuary; identifying birds in the salt marshes; and bumping into former President Jimmy Carter at a seafood restaurant. Listen carefully to the clues, and then draw a line connecting each person with his or her favorite vacation memory.

Clues

1. Sebastian and his mom visited the beach at low tide and also visited turtle sanctuary.
2. Grandma Tonia loved sitting on the balcony early in the morning, when the birds become active in the marshes.
3. Becky is not the person whose favorite memory was the turtle sanctuary.

The Birthday Album

Dakota, Taylor, Logan, and Jackson are making a combined birthday album-scrapbook. Each friend contributes photos and mementos from his or her birthday, held at one of the following places: the Water Park; the Bouncing Air Arcade; the Magic Park; and the Victorian Doll Museum. Listen carefully to the clues, and then draw a line connecting each person to his or her birthday celebration.

Clues

1. Dakota and the girl who celebrated at the quaint tearoom and the adjoining Victorian Doll Museum invited both boys and girls to their parties.
2. Jackson and the boy who loved bouncing at the Air Arcade both celebrate birthdays during the same month.
3. Dakota is not the person who celebrated at the Magic Park.

Lesson 30

Lavender Farm

Chloe, Kaitlyn, Aidan, and London visit the Lavender Farm. They all spend a wonderful afternoon there. Each person leaves with a different favorite memory: gathering bundles of lavender; sampling lavender lemonade and jelly; crafting lavender wreaths; and making lavender cookies. Listen carefully to the clues, and then draw a line connecting each person with his or her favorite Lavender Farm memory.

Clues

1. Chloe and the girl who spent most of her time gathering lavender planned to make sachets for gifts.
2. Aidan and the boy who enjoyed the lavender lemonade and jelly were amazed at how gentle the honeybees were that worked in the lavender fields among the people gathering the wonderful smelling stems.
3. Chloe is **not** the person who enjoyed making lavender cookies.

Landon   Aidan

Chloe   Kaitlyn

County Fair

Shannon, Tasha, Colby, and Adam attend the county fair near their homes. While wandering the fairgrounds, they each have a different favorite activity: fishing for prizes; going down the giant slide; eating funnel cake; and putting golf balls at a target. Listen carefully to the clues, and then draw a line connecting each person to his or her favorite county fair activity.

Clues

1. Colby and the boy who could putt golf balls through a narrow opening stayed for the evening fireworks.
2. Shannon and the girl who loved fishing for plastic ducks to win prizes had 25 tickets each.
3. Colby did not like the funnel cake.

Adam

Colby

Shannon

Tasha

Pattern Decoding

Lessons 32–39

Draw a line to the thing that should come next in each pattern.

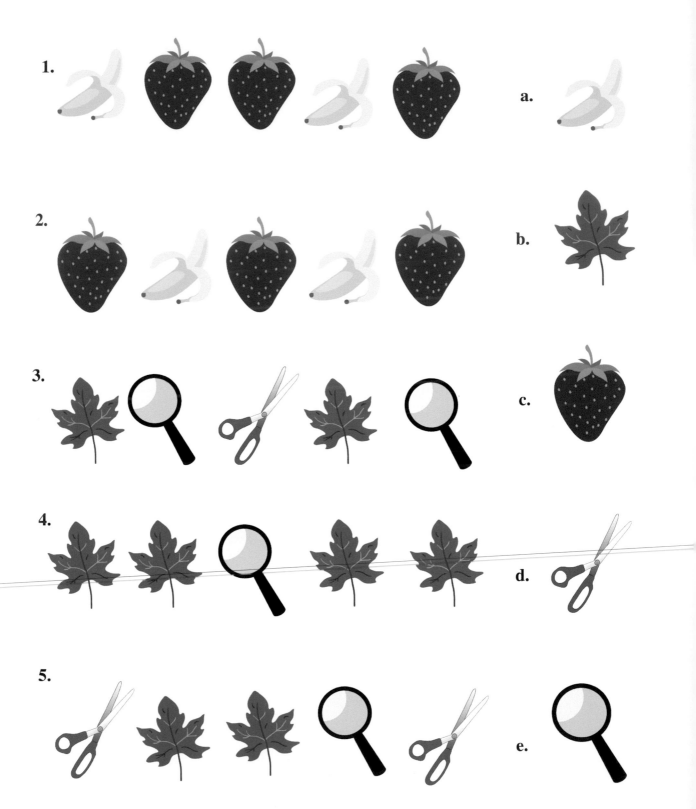

DOI: 10.4324/9781003387213-5

Lesson 33

Draw a line to the thing that should come next in each pattern.

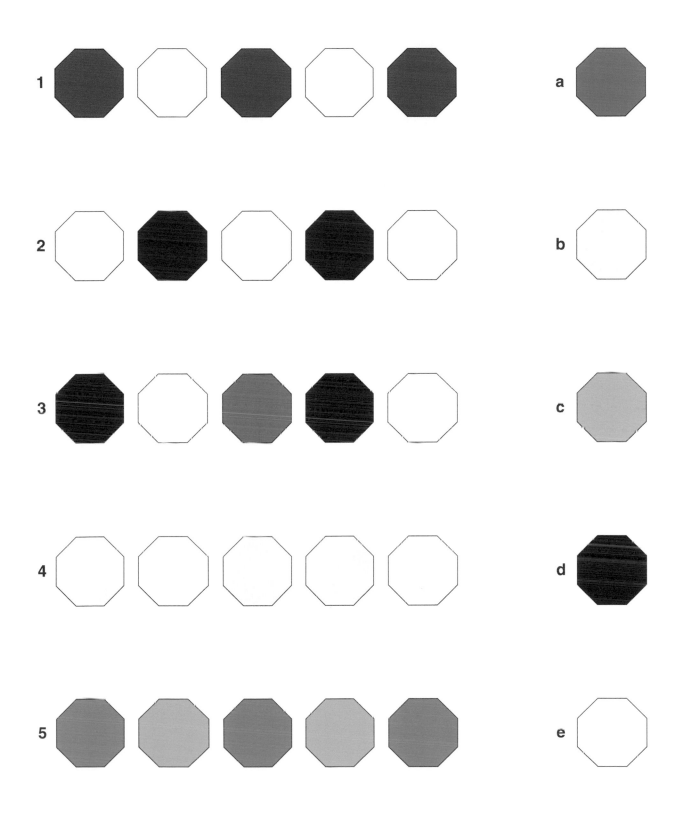

Lesson 34

Draw a line to the thing that should come next in each pattern.

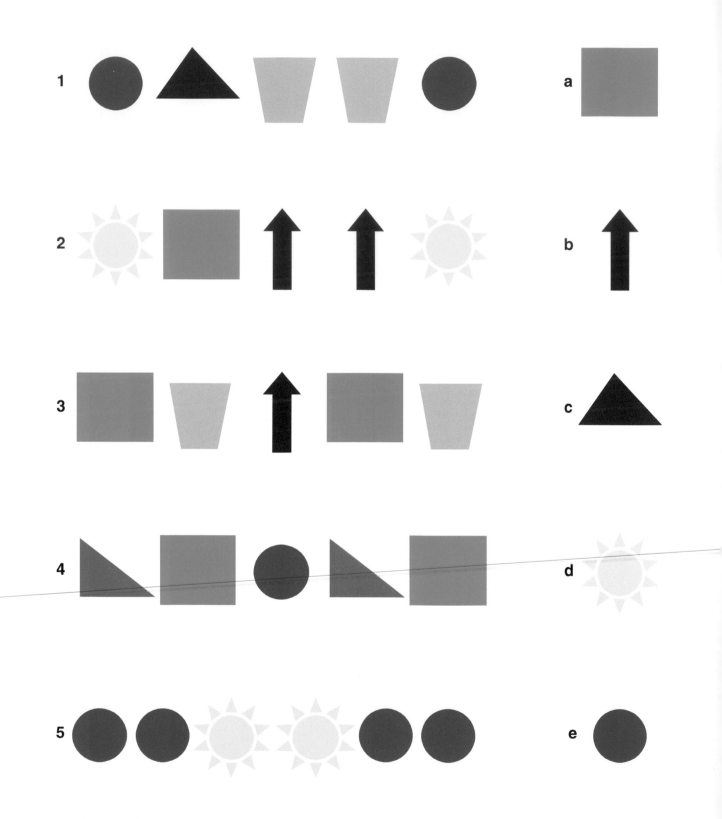

Draw a line to the thing that should come next in each pattern.

1.   a.

2.   b.

3.   c.

4.   d.

5.   e.

Draw a line to the thing that should come next in each pattern.

Draw a line to the thing that should come next in each pattern.

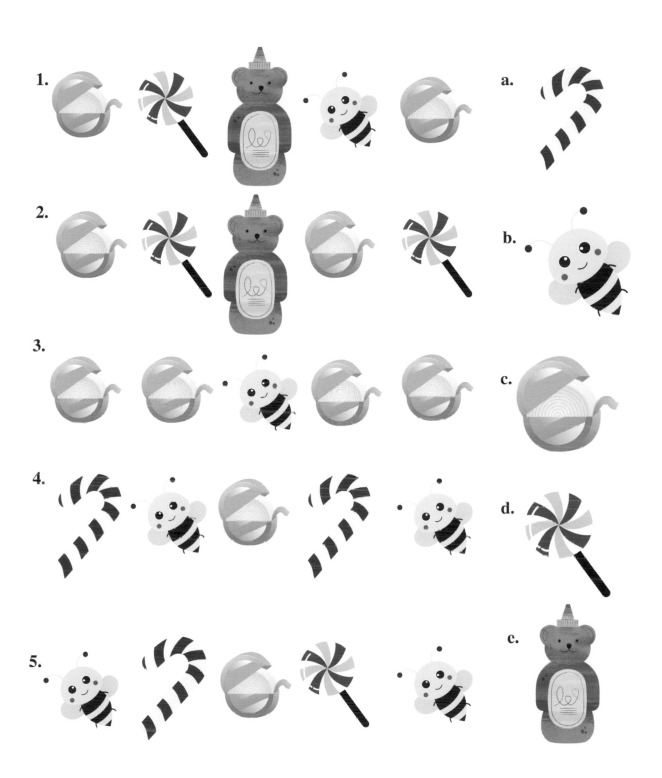

Draw a line to the thing that should come next in each pattern.

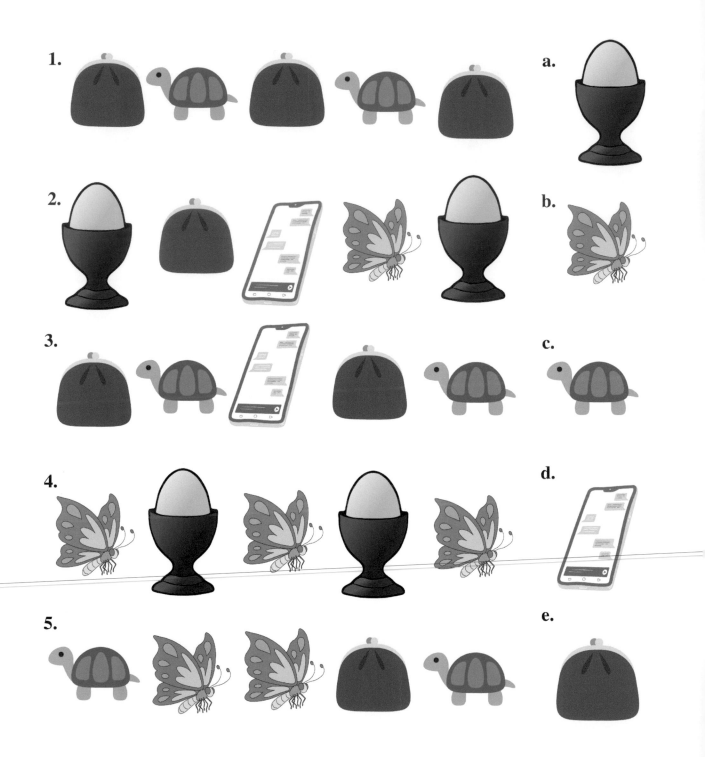

Draw a line to the thing that should come next in each pattern.

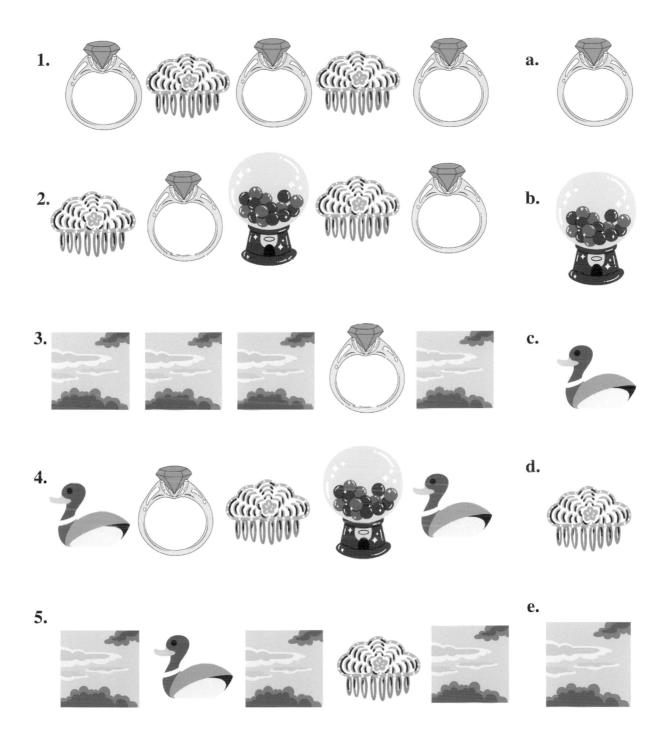

Inference

Lessons 40–49

Lesson 40

Draw a line between each picture and the piece that would fit with it to make a complete picture.

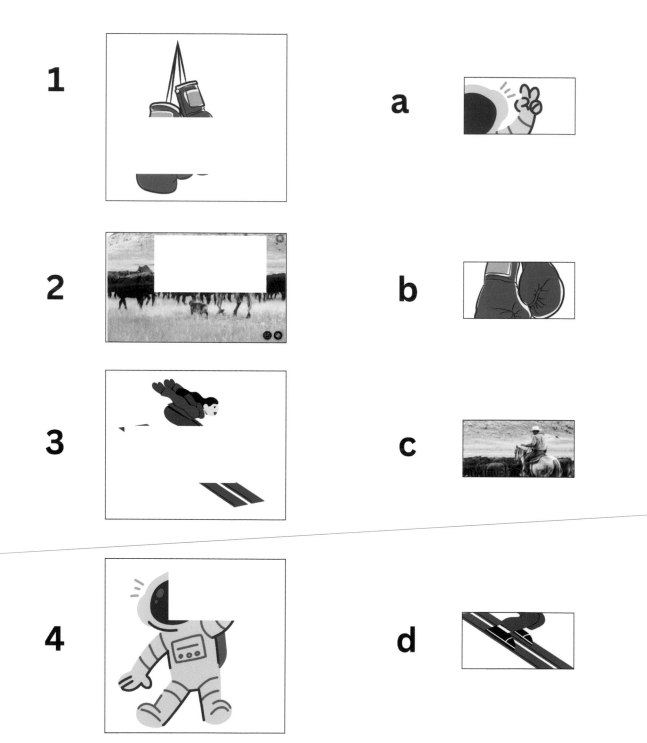

1

a

2

b

3

c

4

d

 DOI: 10.4324/9781003387213-6

Draw a line between each picture and the piece that would fit with it to make a complete picture.

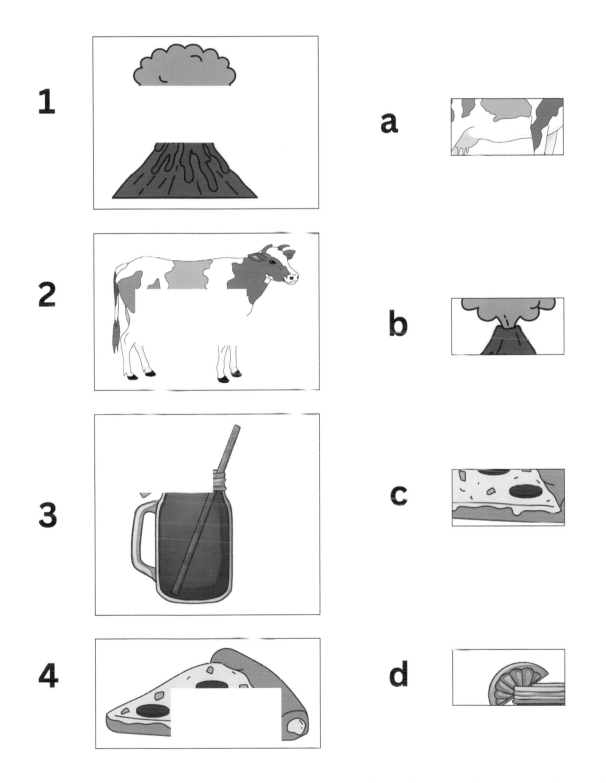

Find the correct missing piece to complete each picture. Draw a circle around it.

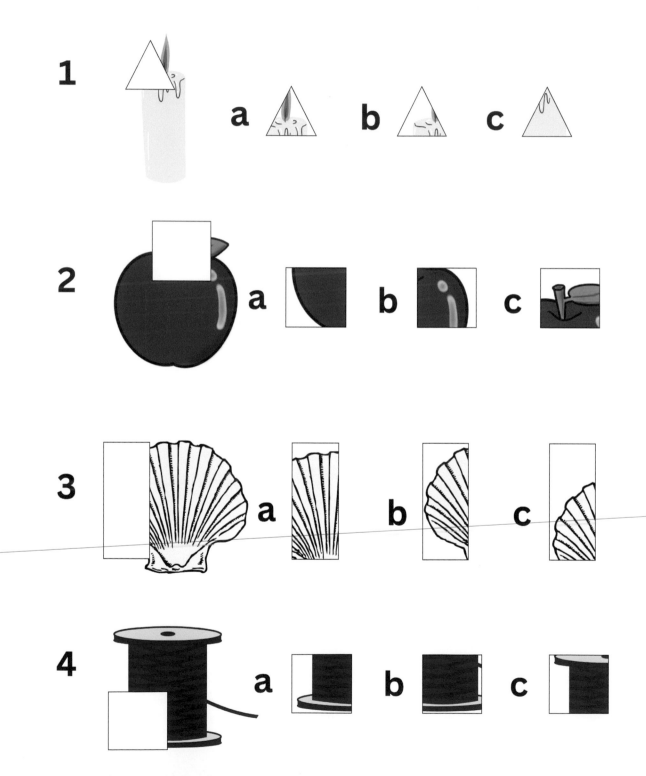

1   a   b   c

2   a   b   c

3   a   b   c

4   a   b   c

Find the correct missing piece to complete each picture. Draw a circle around it.

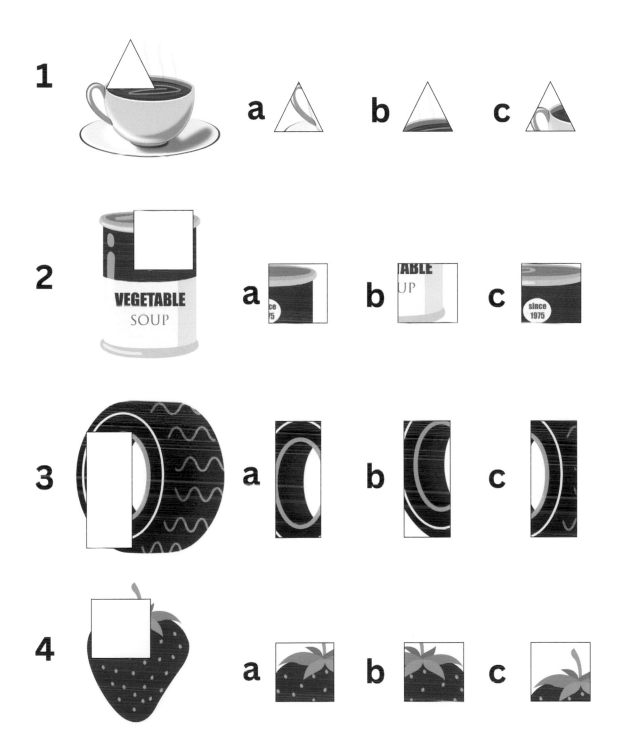

Look at the puzzle pieces. Decide what picture is on the puzzle. Draw it on a separate piece of paper.

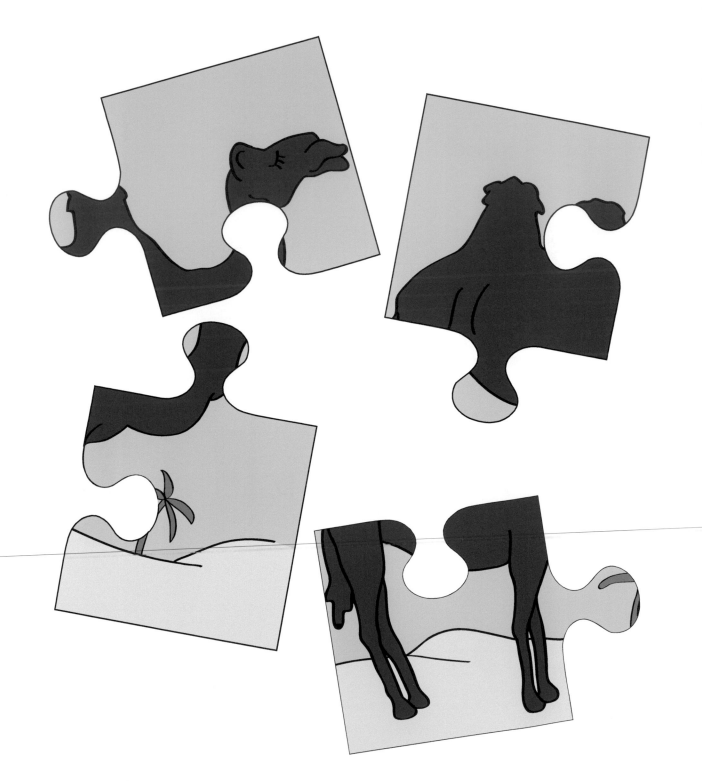

Lesson 45

Look at the puzzle pieces. Decide what picture is on the puzzle. Draw it on a separate piece of paper.

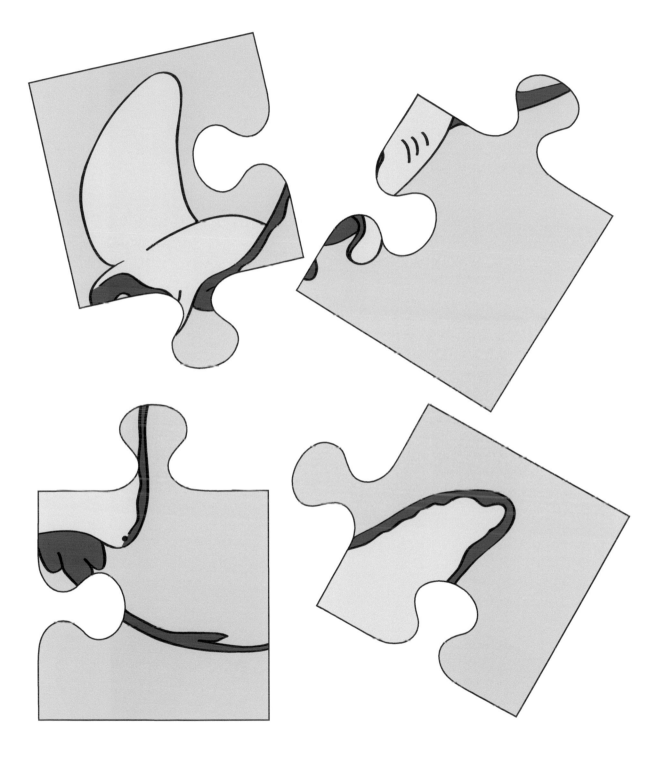

Draw a line to connect the pictures that go together.

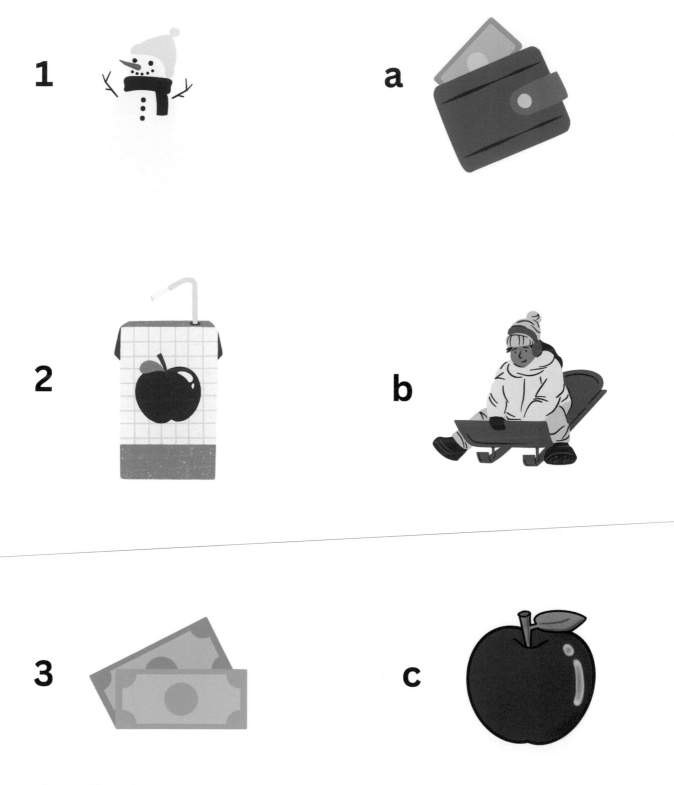

1

a

2

b

3

c

Draw a line to connect the pictures that go together.

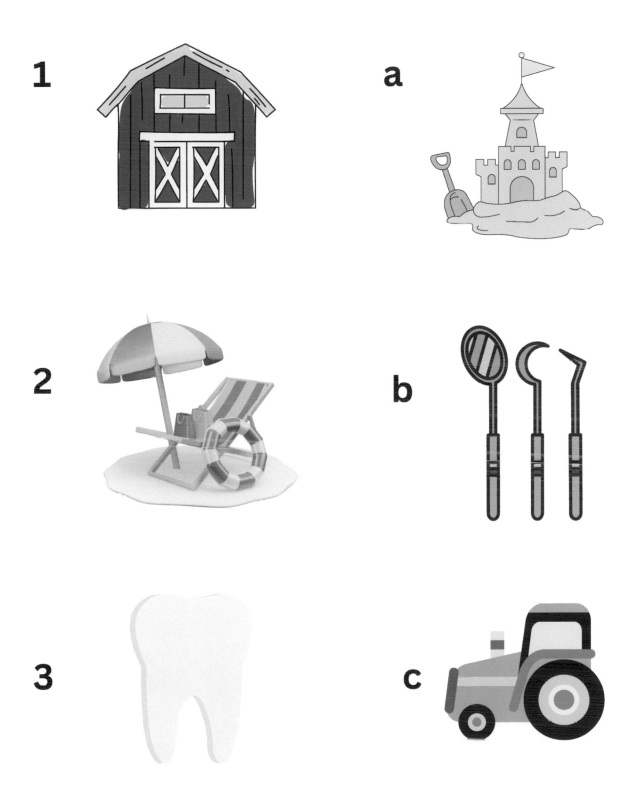

Can you guess what these pictures are?

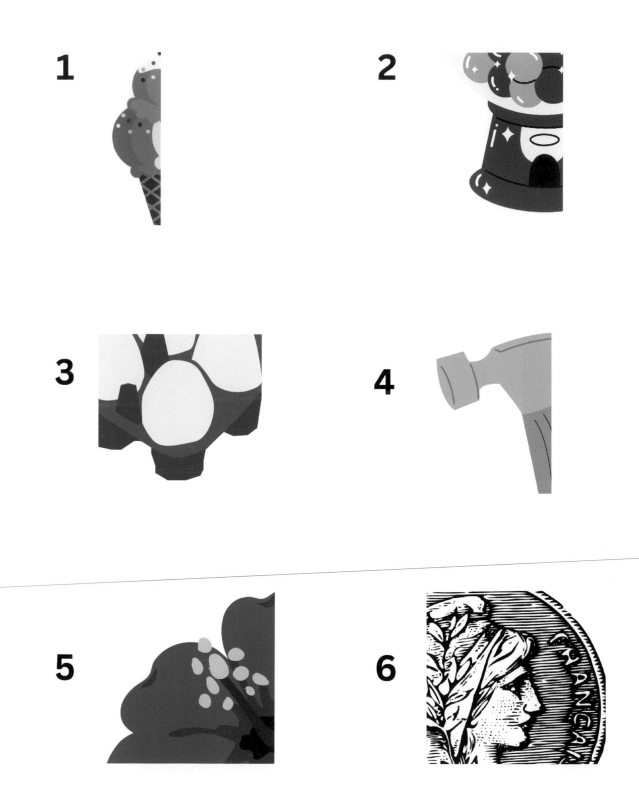

Can you guess what these pictures are?

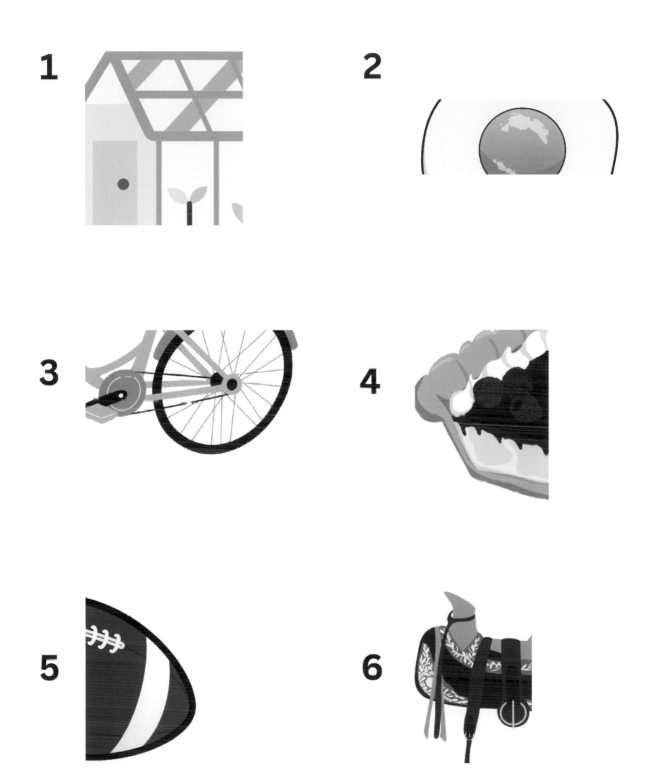

1

2

3

4

5

6

Critical Analysis

Lessons 50–52

Lesson 50

Critical Analysis

These are leemoys.

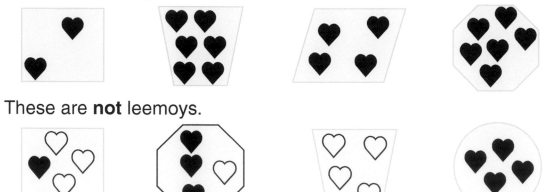

These are **not** leemoys.

Draw a **circle** around all of these things that **are** leemoys.
Draw an **X through** all of the things that are **not** leemoys.

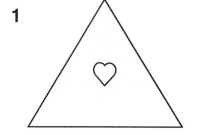

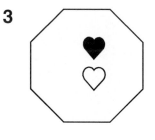
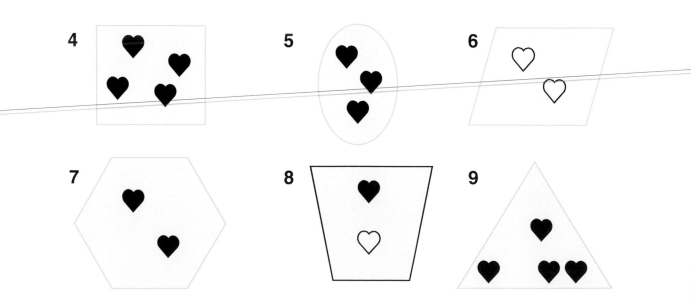

 DOI: 10.4324/9781003387213-7

These are shootles.

These are **not** shootles.

Draw a **circle** around all of these things that **are** shootles.

Draw an **X through** all of the things that are **not** shootles.

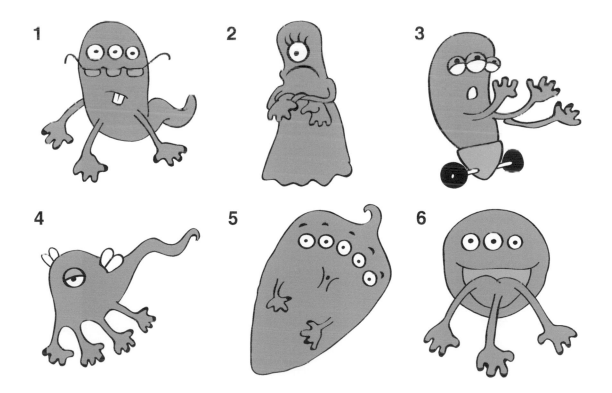

These are beltazoids.

  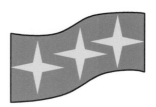

These are **not** beltazoids.

Draw a **circle** around all of these things that **are** beltazoids.
Draw an **X through** all of the things that are **not** beltazoids.

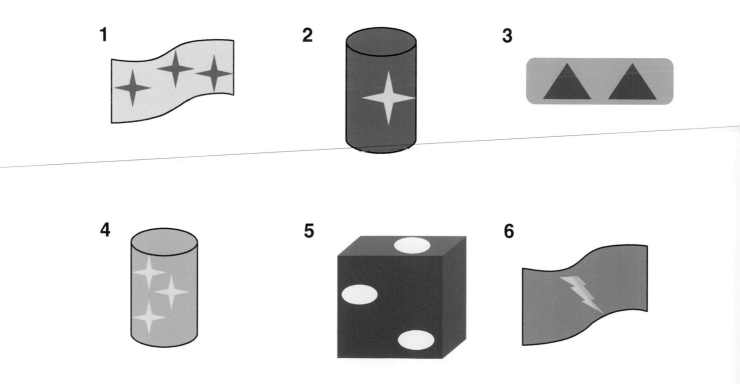

1

2

3

4

5

6

Answers

Lesson 1
1. f
2. c
3. d
4. b
5. e
6. a

Lesson 2
1. d
2. c
3. b
4. a
5. f
6. e

Lesson 3
1. a
2. d
3. b
4. c
5. e
6. f

Lesson 4
1. c
2. a
3. e
4. f
5. d
6. b

Lesson 5
1. e
2. b
3. c
4. d
5. a
6. f

Lesson 6
1. c
2. f
3. a
4. d
5. e
6. b

Lesson 7
1. a
2. f
3. b
4. c
5. e
6. d

Lesson 8
1. d
2. f
3. e
4. c
5. a
6. b

Lesson 9
1. c
2. b
3. b
4. c
5. a

Lesson 10
1. b
2. b
3. c
4. b
5. b

Lesson 11
1. b
2. a
3. c
4. a
5. a

Lesson 12
1. b
2. a
3. c
4. c
5. a

Lesson 13
Circles: 1, 3, 4, 5, 7
X: 2, 6, 8, 9, 10

Lesson 14
Circles: 2, 3, 5, 7, 9, 10
X: 1, 4, 6, 8

Lesson 15
Circles: 2, 3, 5, 6, 8, 10
X: 1, 4, 7, 9

Lesson 16
Circles: 1, 2, 5, 6, 7, 8, 10
X: 3, 4, 9

Lesson 17
1. b
2. b
3. c
4. b
5. a

Answers

Lesson 18
1. b   4. b
2. a   5. a
3. c

Lesson 19
1. b   4. c
2. a   5. b
3. b

Lesson 20
1. b   3. a
2. c   4. b

Lesson 21
1. c   3. c
2. b   4. c

Lesson 22
1. b   3. c
2. c   4. b

Lesson 23
1. c   3. b
2. c   4. a

Lesson 24
1. b   3. c
2. a   4. a

Lesson 25
Sebastian: Sushi
Evan: Pot stickers
Emma: Noodle Soup
Falon: Shrimp fried rice

Lesson 26
Rob: Hummingbird green/red velvet
Tyler: Mulberry purple/jack-o-lantern orange
Sydney: Swallowtail yellow/cedar green
Lydia: Watermelon pink/robin's-egg blue

Lesson 27
Nick: String cheese
Clayton: Juice pouches
Crystal: Strawberry leather
Julie: Apple slices

Lesson 28
Grandma Tonia: Birds in salt marshes
Grandpa Dave: Former president Jimmy Carter
Becky: Collecting shells
Sebastian: Turtle sanctuary

Lesson 29
Logan: Bouncing Air Arcade
Jackson: Magic Park
Dakota: Water Park
Taylor: Victorian Doll Museum

Lesson 30
Aidan: Making lavender cookies
Landon: Sampling lemonade and jelly
Chloe: Crafting lavender wreaths
Kaitlyn: Gathering bundles of lavender

Lesson 31
Colby: Going down the giant slide
Adam: Putting golf balls
Shannon: Eating funnel cake
Tasha: Fishing for prizes

Lesson 32
1. c   4. e
2. a   5. b
3. d

Lesson 33
1. e   4. b
2. d   5. c
3. a

Lesson 34
1. c   4. e
2. a   5. d
3. b

Lesson 35
1. a   4. e
2. d   5. c
3. b

Lesson 36
1. d   4. b
2. c   5. e
3. a

Lesson 37
1. d   4. c
2. e   5. a
3. b

Lesson 38
1. c   4. a
2. e   5. b
3. d

Lesson 39
1. d   4. a
2. b   5. c
3. e

Lesson 40
1. b   3. d
2. c   4. a

Lesson 41
1. d   3. b
2. c   4. a

Lesson 42
1. b   3. a
2. b   4. a

Lesson 43
1. a   3. a
2. c   4. b

Lesson 44
Camel

Lesson 45
Sting ray

Lesson 46
1. b   3. a
2. c

Lesson 47
1. c   3. b
2. a

Lesson 48
1. Sundae   4. Hammer
2. Bubblegum machine   5. Flower
3. Egg carton   5. Coin

Lesson 49
1. Greenhouse   4. Cherry pie
2. Egg   5. Football
3. Bicycle   5. Saddle

Lesson 50
Leemoys are unshaded geometric figures with all straight sides enclosing an even number of shaded objects. Circle 2, 4, 7, and 9.

Lesson 51
Shootles are creatures that do not have the same number of eyes as they have hands. Circle 2, 4, and 5.

Lesson 52
Beltazoids are figures with one or more stars on them. Circle 1, 2, and 4.

Common Core State Standards Alignment Sheet
Lollipop Logic (Book 2)

Lesson	Common Core State Standards
Sequences (Lessons 1–8)	**Math** CCSS.MATH.CONTENT.K.CC.B.4.A When counting objects, say the number names in the standard order, pairing each object with one and only one number name and each number name with one and only one object. CCSS.MATH.CONTENT.K.CC.B.4.C Understand that each successive number name refers to a quantity that is one larger.
Relationships (Lessons 9–16)	**ELA-Language** CCSS.ELA-LITERACY.L.K.5 With guidance and support from adults, explore word relationships and nuances in word meanings. CCSS.ELA-LITERACY.L.1.5 With guidance and support from adults, demonstrate understanding of word relationships and nuances in word meanings.
Analogies (Lessons 17–24)	**Math** CCSS.MATH.CONTENT.K.G.B.4 Analyze and compare two- and three-dimensional shapes, in different sizes and orientations, using informal language to describe their similarities, differences, parts (e.g., number of sides and vertices/"corners") and other attributes (e.g., having sides of equal length). CCSS.MATH.CONTENT.1.G.A.1 Distinguish between defining attributes (e.g., triangles are closed and three-sided) versus non-defining attributes (e.g., color, orientation, overall size); build and draw shapes to possess defining attributes. **ELA-Language** CCSS.ELA-LITERACY.L.K.5 With guidance and support from adults, explore word relationships and nuances in word meanings. CCSS.ELA-LITERACY.L.1.5 With guidance and support from adults, demonstrate understanding of word relationships and nuances in word meanings.

Lesson	Common Core State Standards
Deduction **(Lessons 25–31)**	**ELA –** CCSS.ELA-LITERACY.RF.K.1; CC.SS.ELA-LITERACY.RF.1.1 Demonstrate understanding of the organization and basic features of print. CCSS.ELA-LITERACY.RF.K.2; CC.SS.ELA-Literacy.RF.1.2 Demonstrate understanding of spoken words, syllables, and sounds (phonemes). CCSS.ELA-LITERACY.RF.K.3; CC.SS.ELA-Literacy.RF.1.3; CC.SS.ELA-Literacy.RF.2.3 Know and apply grade-level phonics and word analysis skills in decoding words. CCSS.ELA-LITERACY.RF.1.4; CCSS.ELA-LITERACY.RF.2.4 Read with sufficient accuracy and fluency to support comprehension.
Pattern Decoding **(Lessons 32–39)**	**Math** CCSS.MATH.CONTENT.4.OA.C.5 Generate a number or shape pattern that follows a given rule. Identify apparent features of the pattern that were not explicit in the rule itself.
Critical Analysis **(Lessons 50–52)**	**Math** CCSS.MATH.CONTENT.K.CC.B.4 Understand the relationship between numbers and quantities; connect counting to cardinality. CCSS.MATH.CONTENT.K.CC.C.6 Identify whether the number of objects in one group is greater than, less than, or equal to the number of objects in another group, e.g., by using matching and counting strategies. CCSS.MATH.CONTENT.K.G.B.4 Analyze and compare two- and three-dimensional shapes, in different sizes and orientations, using informal language to describe their similarities, differences, parts (e.g., number of sides and vertices/"corners") and other attributes (e.g., having sides of equal length). CCSS.MATH.CONTENT.1.G.A.1 Distinguish between defining attributes (e.g., triangles are closed and three-sided) versus non-defining attributes (e.g., color, orientation, overall size); build and draw shapes to possess defining attributes.

Image Credits

Lesson 1
Shutterstock

Lesson 2
Shutterstock

Lesson 3
Shutterstock

Lesson 5
Shutterstock

Lesson 6
Shutterstock

Lesson 9
Image of Hamburger by Clker-Free-Vector-Images from Pixabay
Hand-drawn Kids Kite ©Sketchify Education via Canva.com
Diamond Ring ©Sketchify via Canva.com
Image of Hot Dog Sandwich by Raka C. from Pixabay
Dinosaur gradient icon ©Eucalyp via Canva.com
Cute Baby Dinosaur ©Sketchify via Canva.com
Image of Sun by OpenClipart-Vectors from Pixabay
Mexican Frog Alebrije ©Ale Rodriguez via Canva.com
Textured Pasta with Meatballs ©Sketchify via Canva.com
Turkey Ebru Lotus Flowers ©Sketchify Turkey via Canva.com
Candle ©itzel morales zurita via Canva.com
Wooden Spoon ©musbila via Canva.com
Science and Research Element Light Bulb ©Sketchify via Canva.com
Cute Cartoon Cat ©Sketchify via Canva.com
Chef's Knife Kitchen Utensils Illustration ©Drawcee zurita via Canva.com
Iced Pink Lemonade Pitcher ©Sketchify via Canva.com
Iced Pink Lemonade ©Sketchify via Canva.com
Image of Cheese by Ryan F from Pixabay
Paintbrush ©Canva Creative Studio via Canva.com

Lesson 10
Mexican Lotery Conch ©ellacamposr via Canva.com
Wooden Bird House ©Tish Studio via Canva.com
Orange Textured Stamp Sea Shell ©Sketchify via Canva.com
Cute Cartoon Cat ©Sketchify via Canva.com

Snowflake Image by Gerd Altmann from Pixabay
Handdrawn Vector Happy Dolphin ©Dorothy Livelo via Canva.com
Snowman Image by Htc Erl from Pixabay
Eggs in a Carton ©sparklestroke via Canva.com
Space Earth Planet Flat Style Icon ©iconsy via Canva.com
Chick bird Image by Clker-Free-Vector-Images from Pixabay
Dragonfly Image by Roger YI from Pixabay
Space Moon Flat Style Icon ©iconsy via Canva.com
Elephant Image by Clker-Free-Vector-Images from Pixabay
Cute Deco Heart Sticker ©sparklestroke via Canva.com
Organic Semi-Lined Giraffe ©Chloe Gaw via Canva.com
Rumah ©Era Giovani via Canva.com
open mailbox with raised flag ©Twemoji via Canva.com
Hand Made Stationery Scissors ©Sketchify via Canva.com
Brown Envelope ©aljon via Canva.com
Cupcake Image by Pintera Studio by Pixabay

Lesson 11

Hen gradient icon ©Eucalyp via Canva.com
Airmail Envelope ©Fusion Books via Canva.com
hatching chick ©Twemoji via Canva.com
Isolated Toothpaste and Brush Icon Flat Design ©iconsy via Canva.com
Pastel Birthday Cake Image by Clker-Free-Vector-Images from Pixabay
Birthday Party Hat Image by Asad Nazir from Pixabay
Emoticon Style Bathtub ©Mer Mendoza via Canva.com
Snake Flat Icon ©Maxicons via Canva.com
Banjo ©Twemoji via Canva.com
Polar Bear Image by Clker-Free-Vector-Images from Pixabay
"Love You" Candy Heart ©Canva Layouts via Canva.com
Trumpet Image by Clker-Free-Vector-Images from Pixabay
Round Acorn Illustration ©Sketchify via canva.com
Squirrel Image by Harshal from Pixabay
Gold Star Image by OpenClipart-Vectors from Pixabay
Flat Map Skills Volcano ©Sketchify Education via Canva.com
Hot Dog Image by Królestwo_Nauki from Pixabay
Sandwich Image by Clker-Free-Vector-Images from Pixabay
Lotus Flower Image by Photography and graphic design by Pixabay
Cute Organic Thermometer ©Sketchify Education via Canva.com

Lesson 12

Fire Extinguisher Image by Satheesh Sankaran from Pixabay
Sleek Isometric Airplane ©M.Wallflower via Canva.com
Lined Geometric Fire Truck ©Sketchify via Canva.com
New YorkElement-14 ©Statement Goods via Canva.com

Pink Shiny Gumball Machine ©Sketchify via Canva.com
Crayon ©Twemoji via Canva.com
Toothbruch ©Twemoji via Canva.com
Bastille Day Themed Sneakers ©Sparklestroke Global via Canva.com
Horse gradient icon ©Eucalyp via Canva.com
Sunset Hot Fill Style Icon ©iconsy via Canva.com
Flat Feet Illustration ©Marx Fidel via Canva.com
Risograph Print Preschool Hot Air Balloon Logo ©Sketchify via Canva.com
Printable Outlined Milk Carton ©sparklestroke via Canva.com
White Cat Image by Clker-Free-Vector-Images from Pixabay
Airplane ©Twemoji via Canva.com
Teepee Image by OpenClipart-Vectors from Pixabay
Traffic Cone Image by Luiz Fernando Vicente Da Silva Fernando from Pixabay
Diamond Ring Illustration Image by Królestwo_Nauki from Pixabay
Pig Image by Królestwo_Nauki from Pixabay

Lesson 13

Socks ©Retnoutari via Canva.com
Skirt Image by Raka C. from Pixabay
Handdrawn Cutout Heels ©Trendify via Canva.com
Jeans Image by OpenClipart-Vectors from Pixabay
Detailed Handdrawn Cap ©Sketchify via Canva.com
Summer Sandals Image by Clker-Free-Vector-Images from Pixabay
T-Shirt Icon ©Macrovector via Canva.com
Indian Flag Color kite vector illustration ©Mete-X via Canva.com
Floppy Sun Hat ©Canva via Canva.com
Tennish shoe Image by OpenClipart-Vectors from Pixabay
Floral Dress Image by OpenClipart-Vectors from Pixabay
Ice cream Image by Pintera Studio by Pixabay
Lined Gradient Pajamas ©Diego Solas via Canva.com
Hippopotamus Image by Clker-Free-Vector-Images from Pixabay
Kawaii Handdrawn Birthday Cake ©Sketchify via Canva.com
Bicycle Image by Yvette W from Pixabay

Lesson 14

Handdrawn Textured Organic LGBTQ+ Roller Skates ©Trendify via Canva.com
Buildable Hand-drawn Organic Rag Doll ©Sketchify Education
Beach Ball Image by OpenClipart-Vectors from Pixabay
Painterly Anime Toy Train ©Diversifysketch via Canva.com
Toy Truck Image by Francis Ray from Pixabay
Simple Lined Pinwheel ©Sketchify Education via Canva.com
Woman with Flowers on Hair Illustration ©Seziinha Illustrations
Handdrawn Organic Fire Extinguisher ©Camille Ramos via Canva.com
Baseball Glove Image by Clker-Free-Vector-Images from Pixabay

Cheese Image by Mostafa Elturkey from Pixabay
Organic Children's Toy Bicycle ©Sketchify via Canva.com
Warm Storybook Lemon Iced Tea ©Sketchify Indonesia via Canva.com
Organic Boho Rocking Horse ©Sketchify UAE via Canva.com
Organic Children's Toy Castle Block ©Sketchify via Canva.com

Lesson 15

Watermelon Slice Image by Clker-Free-Vector-Images from Pixabay
Pear Agriculture Block and Flat Icon ©iconsy via Canva.com
Grape Icon ©iconsy via Canva.com
Simple Lined Raspberry ©Sketchify Education via Canva.com
Fruit ©Atdaographic via Canva.com
French horn Image by Clker-Free-Vector-Images from Pixabay
Orange Image by Marta Cuesta on Pixabay
Apple ©Ine Bruckers via Canva.com
nesting dolls ©Twemoji via Canva.com
melon ©wingzky via Canva.com
Cherries Image by Marta Cuesta on Pixabay
Clean Vector Transport Elements School Bus ©Sketchify via Canva.com
Banana ©Twemoji via Canva.com
Buildable Christmas Backgrounds Fireplace ©Sketchify
Strawberry Image by Clker-Free-Vector-Images from Pixabay

Lesson 16

Popcorn Image by 6847478 from Pixabay
Planter Image by OpenClipart-Vectors from Pixabay
measuring gradient icon ©Eucalyp via Canva.com
Organic Semi-Lined Tortoise ©Chloe Gaw via Canva.com
Housekeeping Bucket Illustration ©Drawcee via Canva.com
Organic Relaxed Badminton Shuttlecock ©Sketchify via Canva.com
Takeaway Coffee Cup ©mary Lacgnor's Images via Canva.com
Striped lighthouse Image by Clker-Free-Vector-Images from Pixabay
Tie Flat Icon ©Macrovector via Canva.com
All other images sourced via Shutterstock

Lesson 17

School Glue ©Sketchify via Canva.com
Lined Doodle Tape Dispenser ©Kenji via Canva.com
Kiwi Half ©Sketchify via Canva.com
Simple Bright Hand Drawn Running Shoes ©Sparklestroke Global via Canva.com
Red, Juice Strawberry ©Canva via Canva.com
Cute Sticker Style Sokoke ©Sketchify via Canva.com
Clay Pot Illustration ©irya via Canva.com
Drum ©Twemoji via Canva.com

Rabbit Image by Michael Rühle from Pixabay
Dreamy Painterly Strawberry Cake ©Trendify via Canva.com
Black Cat Image by OpenClipart-Vectors from Pixabay
Organic Children's Toy Jack in a Box ©Sketchify via Canva.com
Toy bricks Image by Clker-Free-Vector-Images from Pixabay
Bright Lined Detailed Halloween Sugary Gummies with Shadows ©Trendify via Canva.com
Colorful Organic Univero ©sparklestroke via Canva.com
Emoticon Style Leaves with Mortar and Pestle ©Mer Mendoza via Canva.com
Lollipop Food Isometric Style Icon ©iconsy via Canva.com
Travel Element Starfish ©Sketchify via Canva.com
Sea Shell Illustration ©lopolitt via Canva.com
Pink Flip Flops ©Denisa Zeqiri via Canva.com
Lined Minimal Arctic Wolf for Tundra Biome Food Web ©Alyssa Babasa via Canva.com
Footwear Colored Textile Soft Slippers Hotel Room Accessories ©ixdesignlab via Canva.com
Watercolor owl, cute illustration ©Natalia Kostenko via Canva.com
Cartoon Wind Turbines on a Field ©Sketchify via Canva.com
Isolated Windmill Icon Flat Design ©iconsy via Canva.com
Iphone ©icons8 via Canva.com
Telephone ©gstudioimagen via Canva.com
Cute Messy Cutout Crab ©Trendify via Canva.com
Simple Geometric Lined Helicopter ©Allan Faustino via Canva.com
Shutterstock

Lesson 18
Polica Hat Security Flat Style Icon ©iconsy via Canva.com
Clean Vector Transport Elements Police Car ©Sketchify via Canva.com
Firefighter Helmet Flat Style Icon ©iconsy via Canva.com
Buildable Christmas Backgrounds (with Outline) Igloo ©Sketchify via Canva.com
Simple Lined Firetruck ©Miathehoooman via Canva.com
Handdrawn Gouache Arabian Oryx ©Sketchify UAE via Canva.com
Fir tree Image by OpenClipart-Vectors from Pixabay
Pinecone Image by Almeida from Pixabay
Apple Tree Illustration Image by LillyCantabile from Pixabay
Shutterstock
Household Cleaning Object Spray Bottle ©Sketchify via Canva.com
Home Garden Wheel Barrow ©Sketchify via Canva.com
Orange Impasto Food Orange ©sparklestroke via Canva.com
Sketchy Patterned Juice ©Sketchify via Canva.com
Peanuts Image by Adam Kusumah from Pixabay
Deer Image by Clker-Free-Vector-Images from Pixabay
Handdrawn Traffic Scooter ©Drawcee via Canva.com
Peanut Butter ©Grocery2 via Canva.com
Handdrawn Organic Piggy Bank ©Camille Ramos via Canva.com
Stack of coins ©djvstock via Canva.com

Pastelcore Household Pillow ©sparklestroke via Canva.com

British Double Decker Bus Photo by OpenClipart-Vectors from Pixabay

Watercolour Feather ©Sketchify via Canva.com

Cartoon Taco Illustration ©Sketchify via Canva.com

Harp Image by Clker-Free-Vector-Images from Pixabay

Detailed Vector Balalaika ©Magtira Paolo via Canva.com

Mexican Sombrero Illustration ©Sketchify via Canva.com

Red Beret ©Canva via Canva.com

Cute Colorful Hand-Drawn Peanut Butter and Jelly Sandwich Breakfast and Snack for Kids ©Sketchify via Canva.com

Kebabs ©Sparklestroke Global via Canva.com

Lesson 19

Magnifying Glass Image by OpenClipart-Vectors from Pixabay

Binoculars ©All Day April via Canva.com

Vector Café Element Toaster ©Sketchify v ia Canva.com

Birdhouse Image by Demet BEKTAŞ from Pixabay

Handdrawn Stove Illustration ©Mikaella Beratio via Canva.com

Saddle gradient icon ©Eucalyp via Canva.com

Melting Ice Cubes Image by HUNG QUACH from Pixabay

Refrigerator Image by OpenClipart-Vectors from Pixabay

Growing Seed Spring Single Element ©Canva via Canva.com

greenhouse gradient icon ©Eucalyp via Canva.com

Christmas Ice Skating Shoe ©Sketchify via Canva.com

Pliers Image by Clker-Free-Vector-Images from Pixabay

Pipe Wrench Image by OpenClipart-Vectors from Pixabay

Women in Builder ©Sketchify via Canva.com

Freeform Gradient Healthcare Stethoscope ©Sketchify via Canva.com

Bread ©pch.vector via Canva.com

Detailed Sketchy Modern Nurse with Vaccine ©Sketchify via Canva.com

Hand-drawn Yellow Canary Bird Exotic Pet ©Sketchify via Canva.com

Watercolor Potato Food Ingredient ©Sketchify via Canva.com

French Fries ©Sketchify via Canva.com

Orange Image by OpenClipart-Vectors from Pixabay

Feather ©Twemoji via Canva.com

Pug Image by Dragan Lukovic from Pixabay

Party Food Juice ©Sketchify via Canva.com

Wedding Couple ©studiog via Canva.com

Flat Textured Clean Round Two Tier Wedding Cake ©Trendify via Canva.com

Old Personal Computer ©Sketchify via Canva.com

Watercolor Cactus Illustration Clipart ©Vivera Design via Canva.com

Mouse Outline Electronic Devices ©Sketchify via Canva.com

Freen avocado icon ©Julia Bilevych via Canva.com

Lesson 20

Bold Industrial and Tech Elements – Cylinder ©sparklestroke via Canva.com
Vegetable Soup ©Grocery2 via Canva.com
Gold Frame ©Vik_Y via Canva.com
Educational Worksheet Geometric Shapes ©sparklestroke via Canva.com
Educational Worksheet Geometric Shapes ©sparklestroke via Canva.com
3D Scene Shapes Blue Cube ©Drawcee via Canva.com
3D Pastel Cube Shape ©Sketchify via Canva.com
Half sun and sea logo line art illustration ©Piixypeach via Canva.com
Sunset on Ocean Illustration ©Vectoryzen via Canva.com
Grape leaves Image by Merethe Liljedahl from Pixabay
Hand Drawn Peach Fruit ©kseniia-g via Canva.com
Chocolate Chip Cookie Image by Tamalee from Pixabay
Tomato Image by OpenClipart-Vectors from Pixabay
Watercolor Italian Food Caprese Salad ©Sketchify via Canva.com
Detailed Traditional Daisy Flower Field ©Sketchify Korea via Canva.com
White Daisy Flower ©Pat Librojo via Canva.com
Label Image by VintageSnipsAndClips from Pixabay
teepee gradient icon ©Eucalyp via Canva.com
Educational Worksheet Geometric Shapes ©sparklestroke via Canva.com
Educational Worksheet Geometric Shapes ©sparklestroke via Canva.com
teepee gradient icon ©Eucalyp via Canva.com
Stop Sign Image by CopyrightFreePictures from Pixabay
Outlined Octagon ©Canva Layouts via Canva.com
Simple Cute Lamp Shade ©Sketchify Korea via Canva.com
Isolated Home Lamp Icon Flat Design ©iconsy via Canva.com
All other images sourced via Shutterstock

Lesson 21

Megaphone Hand Drawn Outline Illustration ©Sketchify via Canva.com
Traffic Cone Illustration Image by Luiz Fernando Vicente Da Silva Fernando from Pixabay
Headphone Self Care Elements ©Sketchify via Canva.com
headphone gradient icon ©Eucalyp via Canva.com
popcorn glass ©Sunny Coloring via Canva.com
Clean Trash Can Image by Clker-Free-Vector-Images from Pixabay
Baseball Glove Drawing Image by Clker-Free-Vector-Images from Pixabay
Baseball Cap ©Canva via Canva.com
Gray Baseball Cap Illustration Image by OpenClipart-Vectors from Pixabay
Graduation Hat ©Canva via Canva.com
American Football ©Twemoji via Canva.com
147794.SVG Image by OpenClipart-Vectors from Pixabay
American Football ©Twemoji via Canva.com
Offset Filled Football Helmet ©Sketchify via Canva.com
Clean rounded vector farm cart ©Sketchify via Canva.com

Image Credits

Illustration of a Tractor Image by OpenClipart-Vectors from Pixabay
Beaver ©Twemoji via Canva.com
Duck ©Twemoji via Canva.com
Stapler ©Fusion Books via Canva.com
567320.png Image by James de Castro James from Pixabay
Dentist gradient icon ©Eucalyp via Canva.com
All other images sourced via Shutterstock

Lesson 22
Bright Slice of Watermelon Image by Clker-Free-Vector-Images from Pixabay
Pineapple ©Atdaographic via Canva.com
Cute Deco Heart Sticker ©sparklestroke via Canva.com
Cute Deco Heart Sticker ©sparklestroke via Canva.com
Textured Flat Circle Donut ©Sketchify Education via Canva.com
Strawberry Sundae in Glass ©Sketchify via Canva.com
Simple Wheel Illustration ©Ali Datuin via Canva.com
Hand Drawn Giant Anteater ©Sparklestroke Global via Canva.com
Cowboy Hat Illustration ©Lera Feeva via Canva.com
Hand Drawn Armadillo ©Eucalyp via Canva.com
Cute Organic Hard Hat ©Sparklestroke Global via Canva.com
Warm Storybook Scattered Coffee Beans ©Sketchify Indonesia via Canva.com
LNY Soft Illustrative Zociac Dragon ©Isen Alejo via Canva.com
Cute Organic Hard Hat ©Sparklestroke Global via Canva.com
Sleek Duotone Construction Crane ©Sketchify via Canva.com
Eggs gradient icon ©Eucalyp via Canva.com
Handdrawn Bird Illustration ©Sketchify via Canva.com
Handdrawn Bird Illustration ©Sketchify via Canva.com
Cute Beaver Illustration Image by Clker-Free-Vector-Images from Pixabay
Cute Beaver Illustration Image by Clker-Free-Vector-Images from Pixabay
Cute Beaver Illustration Image by Clker-Free-Vector-Images from Pixabay
Eggs gradient icon ©Eucalyp via Canva.com

Lesson 23
Stop Sign Image by CopyrightFreePictures from Pixabay
Yellow School Crossing Street Sign Image by Clker-Free-Vector-Images from Pixabay
Analog Clock Illustration ©Lemuel Taytay via Canva.com
Glacier Image by Darwin Laganzon from Pixabay
Freeform Textured Wildlife Animal Polar Bear ©Sketchify Russia via Canva.com
Down Arrow ©Moudesain via Canva.com
Watercolor Colored Crayons ©Thidabee via Canva.com
Archetype Art Style Tileable Plains Bison ©Trendify via Canva.com
Ramen Image by DuckaHouse from Pixabay
Landscape Scene Beach Flat Style Icon ©iconsy via Canva.com
Pink Crayon ©Sketchify via Canva.com

Crayon ©Twemoji via Canva.com
Australian Huntsman spide Poster Illustration ©sparklestroke via Canva.com
Cute Impasto Animal Duck ©sparklestroke via Canva.com
Crayon Doodle Dog Kennel ©Sketchify via Canva.com
Three Ants Illustration Image by Clker-Free-Vector-Images from Pixabay
Yellow Butterfly vector image Image by OpenClipart-Vectors from Pixabay
Blue Butterfly vector Image by OpenClipart-Vectors from Pixabay
Vector pink balloon with string ©ReallyCreative via Canva.com
Birthday Balloons Clipart ©hnh-nh-ca-noble-okuneva via Canva.com
Pink Flower ©WinnyThePooh via Canva.com
Flower in a Vase Self Care Elements ©Sketchify via Canva.com
Lined Psychedelic Groovy Daffodil Flower Illustration ©Sketchify via Canva.com
eel gradient icon ©Eucalyp via Canva.com
Psychedelic Surrealism Stylized Animal Balloon ©Max Reyes via Canva.com
Old Gramophone Player ©Drawcee via Canva.com
All other images sourced via Shutterstock

Lesson 24

Up Arrow Icon ©APWP via Canva.com
Down Arrow Icon ©APWP via Canva.com
39526.svg Image by Clker-Free-Vector-Images from Pixabay
39526.svg Image by Clker-Free-Vector-Images from Pixabay
Sunflower Wreath Watercolor ©wannafang via Canva.com
Illustration of a Donut Image by Bianca Van Dijk from Pixabay
46396.svg Image by Clker-Free-Vector-Images from Pixabay
Bread Loaf Vector Image by Clker-Free-Vector Images from Pixabay
Snowboarder Man Illustration ©Drawcee via Canva.com
Cute Winter Snowman ©Scoffer via Canva.com
Cherry Pie Illustration Image by OpenClipart-Vectors from Pixabay
Cherry Fruit Image by OpenClipart-Vectors from Pixabay
Vibrant Simplified Paper Cutout Guinea Pig ©Aisha Villabona via Canva.com
Abstract Organic Animal Full Body Nandu ©Sketchify Argentina via Canva.com
World globe single isolated object ©ribkhan via Canva.com
Hand drawn Marble Mexican Toy ©Flore Dis via Canva.com
Arthropod Vector Image by OpenClipart-Vectors from Pixabay
World globe single isolated object ©ribkhan via Canva.com
Bee Hive Illustration Image by anns from Pixabay
Pizza ©heavylogo via Canva.com
Peanuts Vector Illustration Image by Adam Kusumah from Pixabay
All other images sourced via Shutterstock

Lesson 25

Fortune Cookie ©Twemoji via Canva.com
Chopsticks ©Twemoji via Canva.com

Chinese Dumpling in Hand drawn style ©Sketchify via Canva.com
Chinese Traditional Food Coloured Yangzhou Fried Rice ©Drawcee via Canva.com
Retro Sushi Set ©Sketchify via Canva.com
Vibrant Textured Flatlay Shoyu Ramen ©Trendify via Canva.com
All other images sourced via Shutterstock

Lesson 26
34917.svg Image by Clker-Free-Vector-Images from Pixabay
watercolor berry ©baddesigner via Canva.com
jack-o-lantern ©Twemoji via Canva.com
Watermelon ©Mikaella Beratio via Canva.com
Yellow Butterfly vector image Image by OpenClipart-Vectors from Pixabay
Christmas Cedar Ornament ©Sketchify via Canva.com
All other images sourced via Shutterstock

Lesson 27
beverage box ©Twemoji via Canva.com
All other images sourced via Shutterstock

Lesson 28
Lined Citypop Inspired Chinese Egret ©Mer Mendoza via Canva.com
Buildable Beach Scenes Seashells and Starfish ©Jea Gavina via Canva.com
Hand Drawn Turtle ©Sketchify via Canva.com
All other images sourced via Shutterstock

Lesson 30
Lavender Icon ©Artnivora Studio via Canva.com
Fully Lined Quirky Vareneye ©Sketchify Russia via Canva.com
Pink Lemonade Drink ©Drawcee via Canva.com
Galletas Cookies Illustration ©Sketchify Mexico via Canva.com
All other images sourced via Shutterstock

Lesson 32
banana ©Twemoji via Canva.com
Handdrawn organic Maple leaf ©Sketchify via Canva.com
Spring Strawberry Single Element ©Canva via Canva.com
Scissors Image by Clker-Free-Vector-Images from Pixabay
Magnifying Glass Image by OpenClipart-Vectors from Pixabay

Lesson 35
Organic Children's Toy Pinwheel ©Sketchify via Canva.com
Organic Children's Toy Jack in a Box ©Sketchify via Canva.com
Beach ball Image by OpenClipart-Vectors from Pixabay

Teddy Bear Image by rai_dn03 from Pixabay
Organic Boho Rocking Horse ©Sketchify UAE via Canva.com

Lesson 36
Barnyard Chicken Image by OpenClipart-Vectors from Pixabay
Baby chick ©Twemoji via Canva.com
Hen gradient icon ©Eucalyp via Canva.com
Cute Sticker Style Ragdoll Cat ©Sketchify via Canva.com
Pug Dog ©Fusion Books via Canva.com

Lesson 37
Candy Cane ©Yi Ern CHEW's Images via Canva.com
Cute Bee Illustration ©Nidnann via Canva.com
90s Aesthetic Clean Detailed Objects Rolled Gum ©Sketchify via Canva.com
Lollipop ©akash kumar khosla via Canva.com
Honey Bear Squeeze Bottle ©sparklestroke via Canva.com

Lesson 38
Egg cup © 2013 - 2023 ClipArt Best
Butterfly Image by Królestwo_Nauki from Pixabay
Turtle ©Twemoji via Canva.com
Travel Element Cellphone ©Sketchify via Canva.com
Purse ©Twemoji via Canva.com

Lesson 39
Diamond Ring Illustration Image by Królestwo_Nauki from Pixabay
Pink Shiny Gumball Machine ©Sketchify via Canva.com
Duck ©Twemoji via Canva.com
Retro Vintage Flamenco Dancers Comb ©Sketchify Spain via Canva.com
Flat Organic Cloudscape ©Sketchify via Canva.com

Lesson 40
Offset filled boxing gloves ©Sketchify via Canva.com
Shutterstock
Skier woman illustration ©Drawcee via Canva.com
Cute astronaut making peace sign ©Sketchify Mich Cervantes via Canva.com

Lesson 41
Simple erupting volcano ©Sketchify Education via Canva.com
48434 Image by Clker-Free-Vector-Images from Pixaby
Warm storybook lemon iced tea ©Sketchify Indonesia via Canva.com
Slice of pizza ©Sketchify via Canva.com

Image Credits

Lesson 42
Dia de Muertos Lit Candle ©Sketchify Mexico via Canva.com
Apple ©Ine Bruckers from Dario La Mela via Canva.com
Illustration of a Scallop Image by Clker-Free-Vector-Images from Pixaby
Brown Sewing Thread Illustration ©Myart via Canva.com

Lesson 43
Cup of Coffee Illustration Image by FlowerOFdestiny from Pixaby
Vegetable Soup ©Grocery2 from MW's Images via Canva.com
Stippled Blocky Tire ©Isen Alejo from Sketchify Education via Canva.com
Spring Strawberry Single Element ©Canva via Canva.com

Lesson 46
Vibrant Buildable Element Snowman ©sparklestroke via Canva.com
Apple Juice Box with Logo and Straw Illustration ©Sketchify from sketchify via Canva.com
Banknotes Cash Money Flat Image Style ©iconsy via Canva.com
Wallet Banknote Money Safe Business Organic Drawn ©iconsy via Canva.com
Little Girl on a Sled ©Sketchify from sketchify via Canva.com
Apple ©Ine Bruckers from Dario La Mela via Canva.com

Lesson 47
Sketchy Handdrawn Farm Objects Barn ©Sketchify via Canva.com
Sun beach umbrella with beach chair icon isolated 3d render Illustration ©Xvector from xvector via Canva.com
Tooth ©Canva Creative Cereal via Canva.com
Sand Castle Illustration Image by Królestwo_Nauki from Pixaby
Dentis gradient icon ©Eucalyp from amethyststudio via Canva.com
tractor ©Twemoji via Canva.com

Lesson 48
ice cream icon Image by pinterastudio from Pixaby
pink shiny gumball machine ©Sketchify from sketchify via Canva.com
Eggs in a Carton ©sparklestroke via Canva.com
Father's Day Illustrated Objects Hammer ©sparklestroke via Canva.com
Abstract Organic Maga Flower Head ©Sketchify Argentina via Canva.com
French Coin Illustration Image by OpenClipart-Vectors from Pixaby

Lesson 49
greenhouse gradient icon ©Eucalyp from amethyststudio via Canva.com
Vector Image by zFunx from Pixaby
Handdrawn Traffic Bicyle ©Drawcee from drawcee via Canva.com
Pie Slice Illustration Image by LOKK999 from Pixaby
Illustration of a Football Image by Clker-Free-Vector-Images from Pixaby
Handdrawn Saddle with Embroidery ©tania licea from Tenate Arte via Canva.com